BECOMING THE
VERY BEST

By Mardoche Sidor, MD,
Karen Dubin, PhD, LCSW, and the SWEET Institute

SWEET Institute Publishing
Transformational Books for a Transformational World

Copyright © 2025 by the SWEET Institute
All rights reserved. No part of this book may be reproduced, stored in a retrieval system, or transmitted in any form or by any means—electronic, mechanical, photocopying, recording, or otherwise—without the prior written permission of the publisher, except in the case of brief quotations embodied in critical articles or reviews.

Published by:
SWEET Institute Publishing
New York, NY
www.sweetinstitutepublishing.com

First Edition
Printed in the United States of America

ISBN: 978-1-968105-13-6

Library of Congress Control Number: [pending]

Cover Design by SWEET Institute Publishing
Interior Design and Layout by SWEET Institute Publishing

For bulk orders, permissions, or media inquiries, please contact:
contact@sweetinstitute.com

Unless otherwise noted, all stories and case examples in this book are either fictionalized or used with permission, and identifying details have been changed to protect the privacy of individuals.

SWEET Institute Publishing
Transformational Books for a Transformational World

Dedication

To all who dare to grow,
To those who choose the harder path of transformation over the easier path of comfort,
To the seekers, the strivers, the healers, and the visionaries,
This book is for you.

And to every mentor, teacher, friend, and loved one who reminded us that greatness is not found in perfection,
but in persistence, compassion, and presence—
we dedicate this work with gratitude and love.

Also by the Authors

Mardoche Sidor, M.D.; Karen Dubin, Ph.D., LCSW; with the SWEET Institute

- Journey to Empowerment
- Discovering Your Worth: Everything You Need to Feel Fulfilled
- The Power of Faith: A Harvard-Trained Psychiatrist Speaking on Faith
- The Psychotherapy Certificate Course: The Clinician and Coach Manual (Books 1–3)
- The Anxiety Course: The Workbook
- What's Missing
- NLP for Clinicians
- 50 SWEET Poems: Reflections on Life, Love, and Self
- The Power of Belief: How Ideas Shape Leaders, Nations, and the Future
- The Courage to Care: Stories of Healing, Hope, and the Power of Social Work — Told by Over 50 SWEET Institute Social Workers
- Transforming Team Relationships from the Inside Out: The SWEET Healing Circle for Agencies — Redefining Accountability, Collaboration, and Culture
- Remembering: The Journey Back to the Pre-Conditioned Self
- The Clinician's Mirror: A Story of Projection, Self-Awareness, and Transformation for Clinicians

- The Secret Is in Remembering: Why We Suffer, Why We Forget, and How to Return to Who We Are

- It's All Perfect: What If Nothing in Your Life Was a Mistake?

- Because of Us: Why Outcomes Change When We Do

- Before Anything Else, Validate: The Missing Link in Healing, Leadership, Relationships, and Personal Growth

- Rewriting the Script: The Power of Transforming Inner Dialogue in Oppressed Communities

- Determined to See: A Science-Based and Story-Driven Integration of A Course in Miracles and the Four Layers of Transformation

- Always Enough: The Transformational Power of Unconditional Positive Regard: How to See, Accept, and Elevate Yourself and Others Through the 4 Layers of Transformation

Foreword

By Carrie Miceli, LMSW,
Senior Manager of Training & Professional Development, New York, and Pioneer Member of the SWEET Institute

When I was first introduced to the SWEET Institute, I did not know that I was stepping into a movement that would change the way we think about learning, healing, and transformation. What began as a community of professionals dedicated to growth quickly revealed itself as something far greater: a place where knowledge becomes practice, where practice becomes presence, and where presence becomes change.

In my years as a social worker, manager, educator, and trainer, I have seen countless programs and countless books that promise transformation. Too often, they leave us with more theory than tools, more words than wisdom, more inspiration than integration. What the SWEET Institute has done here is different. This is not simply another book; rather, a map, a compass, and a practice all in one.

The framework of the Four Layers of Transformation—conscious, preconscious, unconscious, and existential—is both timeless and revolutionary. Timeless because it honors the truths that thinkers from Freud to Frankl, from ancient wisdom traditions to modern neuroscience, have always known. Revolutionary because it does what so few models dare: it bridges intellectual understanding with lived experience. It insists that transformation is not about collecting knowledge but about embodying it—moving from theory into action, from intention into integration.

As one of the first members of SWEET, I have witnessed this method in practice with clinicians, leaders, and communities. I have seen what happens when people commit to not just reading about change but living it. I have seen clinicians shift the way they engage, leaders shift the way they lead, and human beings shift the way they see themselves. What this book offers is not just a philosophy; rather, it is a pathway.

You will notice that each chapter follows a rhythm: story, conversation, science, case studies, tools, integration, closing reflection. This rhythm mirrors life itself: the stories that shape us, the dialogues that move us, the science that grounds us, the practices that stretch us, and the reflections that return us home. It is a rhythm that speaks not only to the mind but also to the heart and soul.

Reading this book, you may find yourself pausing—not because you are stuck, but because you are stirred. You may find yourself underlining a sentence that feels less like new information and more like a truth you have always known but forgotten. You may find yourself moved to act differently, to breathe differently, to live differently; and that is the power of this work.

The SWEET Institute is not simply a thought leader. It sets the vision and insists that healing, growth, and greatness are possible for every one of us—not someday, but now. In a world that often confuses noise for wisdom and speed for progress, this book calls us back to what matters: presence, purpose, compassion, and courage.

It is my great honor to introduce this work to you. As you walk through its pages, may you also walk the Circle of Transformation—through habit and discipline, through beliefs and patterns, through shadow and integration, into the freedom of meaning and purpose. May you not only read these words but live them.

This is not just a book. It is an invitation. It is an invitation to become not just good, not just excellent, but the very best version of yourself—for your sake, and for the sake of a world waiting for your light.

Carrie Miceli, LMSW
Senior Manager of Training & Professional Development, CJA New York
Pioneer Member, SWEET Institute

Preface

By Monique Anderson, LMSW, RN
Director of Operations at Healthfirst

As both a nurse and a social worker, I have learned that healing is never one-dimensional. It does not begin and end with medication, therapy, or treatment plans; rather, it begins with people, with presence, and with the courage to see another human being fully and to walk with them through both struggle and possibility.

In my work as Director of Operations at HealthFirst, I have witnessed firsthand the complexity of care. People do not come to us with neat categories; they come with stories, histories, pain, resilience, and dreams. To truly serve them, we must meet them not only with skills and knowledge, but with authenticity, humility, and love.

That is why this book matters. It is not another collection of theories; rather, it is an invitation to transformation, and a layered process that mirrors what I have lived in my own practice and in my own growth. At the SWEET Institute, where I have been proud to be a member, I found a community that insisted on going beyond information into integration. We practiced together, reflected together, and reminded one another that the best clinicians are those who do the inner work while serving outwardly.

For me, the purpose of this book is clear: it is a call to all of us who care, who lead, who dare to make a difference. It is a reminder that greatness is not defined by titles, degrees, or recognition, but by how consistently we align our daily actions with our deeper values.

I believe every page of this book holds the potential to shift not just how you think, but how you live and serve. My hope is that, as you read, you will pause often, not just to understand, but to integrate; and not just to gather knowledge, but to transform.

Because ultimately, being "the very best" is not about arriving somewhere; rather, it is about who we become along the way, and how we use that becoming to uplift the lives of others.

— Monique Anderson, LMSW, RN
Director of Operations at Healthfirst

Introduction: The Path of the Very Best

What makes someone the very best at what they do? Is it talent? Luck? A rare gift reserved for the chosen few? For centuries, greatness has been misunderstood, it has been wrapped in myth, admired from afar, and too often thought to be unattainable. The truth is far simpler, and far more empowering: the very best are not born; rather, they are shaped, layer by layer, choice by choice, moment by moment.

This book is about that shaping. It is about the Circle of Transformation, a framework drawn from psychology, neuroscience, philosophy, and lived human experience. It is a circle because transformation is not linear, and growth is not a one-time ascent; rather, a lifelong return, unfolding to depend on and integrate more each time.

The Four Layers of Transformation

The path begins with four layers, each of which is to be encountered and integrated for true change to occur:

1. The Conscious Layer – Discipline and Daily Practice.

Here, transformation begins with action: new habits, routines, and lifestyle changes, which includes sleep, nutrition, exercise, meditation, and breath. These are the outer practices that set the foundation.

2. The Preconscious Layer – Schemas and Patterns.

Beneath behavior lie beliefs, old scripts, inherited schemas, and stories of inadequacy or fear. At this layer, we learn to see and rewrite them, replacing limitation with possibility.

3. The Unconscious Layer – The Hidden Self.

Deeper still lies what has been repressed: forgotten grief, unspoken shame, unresolved conflict. Transformation here requires the courage to face what has been hidden and bring it into light.

4. The Existential Layer – Freedom, Meaning, and Integration.

At the heart of the circle is freedom: the ability to choose, to create meaning, and to live with purpose. It is here that transformation becomes integration, and life becomes art.

The Circle of Transformation

The four layers together create a circle because we ought to walk it again and again. With each cycle, we grow more grounded in practice, freer in belief, more integrated in self, and more anchored in meaning. The circle reminds us that greatness is not a destination but a way of living.

This book will guide you through that circle; and not with theory alone; rather, with stories, conversations, science, case studies, tools, and reflections. Each chapter follows the same rhythm:

- The Story – a narrative to capture the heart.
- Conversation – a dialogue between the authors, inviting reflection.
- Science – evidence from psychology, neuroscience, and research.
- Case Studies – real-world application.
- Toolbox – practices, prompts, and commitments.
- Integration – linking back to the Four Layers.
- Closing Narrative – a final reflection to carry forward.

Why This Book

Every generation asks itself what it means to live well, to live fully, and to live with purpose. In our time, the question has grown urgent. We live in an age of information without integration, connection without depth, and progress without peace. We know more than ever, yet we are not necessarily living better.

This book exists because knowing is not enough. We do not suffer from a lack of information; rather, from a gap between information and transformation, between reading and doing, and between understanding and becoming.

At the SWEET Institute, we have seen this gap up close. We have worked with clinicians, leaders, and everyday seekers who are overflowing with knowledge yet still feel stuck. They know what they 'should' do, but knowing alone doesn't change lives. What changes lives is moving from the conscious layer of practice, through the preconscious patterns that hold us back, into the unconscious material that demands healing, and finally to the existential freedom of meaning and purpose.

This is why this book is necessary. It is not simply about greatness in the abstract; rather, it is about the very best version of you, brought forward in the real world. It is about bridging research and practice, intellect and action, and theory and life. It is about giving you the tools, reflections, and frameworks to walk the Circle of Transformation again and again until it becomes your way of being.

Why this book? Because greatness is not a luxury; rather, it is a responsibility. The world does not need more people who are merely good; rather, it needs people who are fully alive, fully present, and fully engaged. It needs leaders, healers, innovators, and everyday visionaries who embody the very best, not for their own sake but for the sake of others.

This book is for you, if you are ready to stop collecting knowledge and start living it. It is for you, if you are ready to move beyond information into integration; and it is for you, if you are ready to step into the circle and discover not just what you can achieve, but who you can become.

This is why this book exists. And this is why it is yours.

What This Book Is About

This book is about transformation, and not the shallow kind of change that fades when motivation runs out, but the deep kind of transformation that reshapes who we are, how we live, and what we bring to the world.

It is about discovering what makes the very best stand out, and not because of luck, talent, or privilege, but because of their willingness to commit to growth, to walk through the layers of transformation, and to integrate their learning into life.

At its heart, this book introduces and guides you through the Four Layers of Transformation:

- The Conscious Layer – where habits, discipline, and daily practices anchor growth.
- The Preconscious Layer – where patterns, schemas, and core beliefs are examined and reshaped.
- The Unconscious Layer – where hidden wounds, repressed material, and forgotten truths are brought into light.
- The Existential Layer – where freedom, meaning, and purpose are embraced and lived.

Together, these layers form what we call the Circle of Transformation, a lifelong path that we walk again and again. The circle is not about perfection but about integration, and about living fully at every layer of our being.

This book is also about the virtues that make greatness real: courage, resilience, compassion, presence, wisdom, love, service, and more. Each chapter explores one of these qualities through story, dialogue, science, case studies, and tools, so that you don't just read about greatness; rather, you practice it.

What this book is about, ultimately, is you. It is about offering you a path to live as the very best version of yourself, and not someday, but now. It is about helping you close the gap between who you are and who you are meant to be.

This book is not just about learning; rather, it is about becoming.

How to Read This Book

This book is not meant to be read quickly, like a novel you race through to see how it ends. It is meant to be lived with, practiced, and returned to again and again. Each chapter is both a mirror and a tool, and a way to see yourself more clearly and a way to step further into who you are becoming.

Here are some suggestions as you begin:

1. Read Slowly.

Transformation takes time. Do not rush, pause often, and let the stories, conversations, and reflections work on you. Some pages may need to be reread, not because they are difficult, but because they are alive.

2. Engage Actively.

This is not a passive book. Each chapter includes toolboxes, reflection prompts, and commitments. Treat them as invitations to practice. Write in the margins, journal your answers, and share your reflections with a trusted friend or colleague.

3. Move Between Layers.

Notice where you are drawn. Some chapters may speak to the conscious layer, such as habits and discipline. Others may challenge your preconscious patterns, while some may stir the unconscious, bringing up buried emotions. Others, still, will invite you into the existential, such as questions of meaning and freedom. Follow the circle as it calls to you.

4. Return Often.

The Circle of Transformation is not linear. You may find yourself cycling through chapters at different seasons of life. That is not repetition; rather, it is deepening. Each return will meet you in a new way.

5. Read in Community.

While this book can be read alone, it comes alive in conversation. Read it with colleagues, friends, or a group. Discuss the prompts, share your insights, for transformation is magnified when it is shared.

6. Let It Change You.

This book is not about accumulating knowledge; rather, it is about becoming. If you finish the book and nothing in your life has shifted, then the book has not yet been read. Let it change how you see, how you act, and how you live.

How to read this book? Slowly. With openness. With courage. With the willingness to not just understand but to transform.

This is not just a book you read. It is a book you practice.

How This Book Works

This book has been designed with one clear purpose: to move you from information to transformation. Too many books fill the mind but never touch the heart or shift daily life. We wanted to create a resource that speaks to all four layers of human change—the conscious, preconscious, unconscious, and existential—so that you can not only understand the process but live it.

That is why each chapter follows a deliberate rhythm:

1. The Story – Transformation begins with story. Stories bypass resistance and speak directly to the heart. Each chapter begins with a narrative to awaken imagination and possibility.

2. Conversation – Growth is dialogical. Here, you will find a conversation between the authors, modeling reflection, challenge, and insight. It reminds you that transformation is not solitary; rather, it happens in dialogue with others and with yourself.

3. Science – Transformation must be grounded. Each chapter includes scientific evidence from psychology, neuroscience, sociology, and beyond, so that what inspires you is also supported by what is true and proven.

4. Case Studies – Abstract ideas come alive in real lives. Case studies, drawn from clinical practice, leadership, and everyday experiences, show what transformation looks like in action.

5. Toolbox – Insight without practice fades. Each chapter provides reflection prompts, inquiries, and action steps to bring ideas into daily life. These are not optional extras; rather, they are the bridge from reading to becoming.

6. Integration – Every chapter ties back to the Four Layers of Transformation. This reminds you that growth is never one-dimensional. Whatever the theme, be it courage, gratitude, resilience, it touches every layer of your being.

7. Closing Narrative – Each chapter ends with a reflection, story, or meditation to leave you not just informed, but transformed, and ready to carry the chapter's lesson into the next moment of your life.

The Circle Behind the Structure

This design is intentional. It mirrors the Circle of Transformation itself: from conscious practice (Toolbox), to preconscious insight (Conversation, Case Studies), to unconscious awakening (Story, Reflection), to existential integration (Closing Narrative). Every chapter is a circle, preparing you to walk the larger circle of your life.

In Practice

This means that as you read, you are not just gathering knowledge; rather, you are stepping into a process. If you allow yourself to fully engage, by the time you complete this book you will not only understand what makes the very best, you will already be living it.

How This Book Came About

This book was not born in a single moment. It was born in countless conversations, seminars, case consultations, and circles of reflection. It was born in the meeting of minds and hearts at the SWEET Institute, where clinicians, leaders, and seekers have gathered not only to learn but to transform.

The seed was planted when we noticed a troubling pattern: people were learning more than ever before, taking courses, reading research, attending trainings, yet struggling to translate knowledge into lasting change. Clinicians understood Acceptance and Commitment Therapy, or Motivational Interviewing, or Unconditional Positive Regard, but struggled to embody them in practice. Leaders studied inside out leadership, or emotional intelligence, or mindset, but faltered in moments of crisis. Human beings knew what they wanted but couldn't bridge the gap between intention and action.

We began to ask: What would it take to close that gap? What would it take to move from information to transformation?

The answer emerged slowly, drawn from the worlds of psychology, neuroscience, philosophy, and lived human experience. It crystallized in what we came to call the Four Layers of Transformation—conscious, preconscious, unconscious, and existential. And it took shape through the model of the Circle of Transformation—a path that invites us to return again and again, each time deepening our integration.

The conversations that followed—between colleagues, between teachers and students, between friends—made it clear that this framework resonated because it was not abstract. It described the lived experience of growth. It gave language to what people felt but could not name. It offered a structure for what, deep down, we all knew: that true change is not one-dimensional; rather, it touches behavior, belief, shadow, and spirit.

This book came about because we could no longer keep this framework to ourselves. It belongs to everyone—clinicians seeking to deepen their practice, leaders striving to guide with integrity, and everyday human beings longing to live as the very best version of themselves.

It came about because we believe the world is hungry for more than information. It is hungry for wisdom, for presence, and for love in action.

And it came about because we, too, are walking the circle. We did not write this book as experts speaking down from a mountaintop; rather, we wrote it as fellow travelers, offering what we have been learning, trying to practice, and trying to live.

That is how this book came about: from a shared longing, a collective practice, and a conviction that greatness is not reserved for the few; rather, it is the birthright of us all.

Front Acknowledgements

This book is not the work of two people alone; rather, it is the fruit of a community, of countless conversations, of mentors, colleagues, family, and friends who have walked with us and reminded us of what is possible.

We thank the members of the SWEET Institute—clinicians, leaders, and seekers—whose courage to engage, question, and grow has given life to every page. You are the living proof that transformation is not just theory, but practice.

We thank our colleagues in the fields of psychiatry, psychology, social work, nursing, and beyond, who continue to push the boundaries of what healing and growth can look like.

We thank our families, who have carried us with love, patience, and presence, reminding us that greatness always begins at home.

And we thank every reader—past, present, and future—for daring to walk the Circle of Transformation with us. This book is incomplete without you.

With gratitude,
Mardoche Sidor, MD
Karen Dubin, PhD, LCSW

Prologue: The Whisper of Greatness

It begins as a whisper, and a question that surfaces in the quiet moments: What more is possible? Who might I become if I lived fully into myself?

For some, the whisper comes in youth, as dreams too bold to name. For others, it comes later, after setbacks, losses, or the dull ache of routine. For all of us, the whisper is the same: a call to greatness, and not as the world defines it, but as the soul longs for it.

Greatness is not perfection, and it is not power, nor fame, nor applause. Greatness is presence, the courage to show up fully, the humility to keep learning, and the discipline to keep practicing, the resilience to keep rising, and the love to keep giving.

This book begins where greatness truly begins: within.

It does not matter where you stand today, whether, at the start of your career, in the middle of a storm, or at the height of success. The call to become the very best is not bound by circumstance; rather, it is bound only by willingness, the willingness to walk the Circle of Transformation, again and again, until you live as the fullest version of yourself.

The chapters that follow are not answers but doorways. Each story, conversation, study, and practice is meant to invite you into a deeper encounter with yourself. As you walk, you may find resistance. You may find old stories rising, shadows surfacing, truths you have long avoided; but that is not failure; rather, that is the path, for greatness is not found outside of you; rather, it is remembered within you.

This book is a companion for that remembering. It is a map, a compass, and above all, a mirror. May you then see yourself in its pages, and may you discover the truth that the whisper has been telling you all along: You were meant for more, and you already are more than you know.

Contents

Part I: The Call to Greatness   **29**

  Chapter 1—What Makes The Very Best   30

  Chapter 2—The Myths of Talent and Luck   34

Part II: The Four Layers of Transformation   **37**

  Chapter 3—Conscious Layer: Discipline and Daily Practice   38

  Chapter 4—Preconscious Layer: Schemas and Patterns   42

  Chapter 5—Unconscious Layer: The Hidden Self   46

  Chapter 6— Existential Layer: Freedom, Meaning, and Integration   50

Part III: Becoming Recognized   **55**

  Chapter 7—Uniqueness: Your Irreplaceable Signature   56

  Chapter 8—Consistency: Excellence as a Lifestyle   60

  Chapter 9—Connection: The Human Element   64

  Chapter 10: Resilience and Reinvention   68

Part IV: Living as the Best   **73**

  Chapter 11—The Purpose Beyond Self   74

  Chapter 12—Integration: The Four Layers in Action   78

Part V: The Virtues of Greatness   **83**

  Chapter 13—Legacy: Leaving What Lasts   84

  Chapter 14—Courage: Facing Fear and Acting Anyway   87

  Chapter 15 —Creativity: Innovation as Path to Greatness   90

  Chapter 16—Humility: The Ground of True Excellence   93

Chapter	Title	Page
Chapter 17	Service: Turning Greatness Into Contribution	96
Chapter 18	Presence: Mastering the Now	99
Chapter 19	Love: The Greatest Force in Human Growth	102
Chapter 20	Wisdom: Integrating Knowledge Into Life	105
Chapter 21	Resilience: Rising Strong from Setbacks	108
Chapter 22	Integrity: Living in Alignment with Truth	111
Chapter 23	Curiosity: The Engine of Growth	114
Chapter 24	Discipline: The Structure of Freedom	117
Chapter 25	Gratitude: The Science of Fulfillment	120
Chapter 26	Forgiveness: Healing and Releasing the Past	124
Chapter 27	Hope: Fuel for the Future	127
Chapter 28	Compassion: The Heart of Greatness	130
Chapter 29	Courageous Conversations: Speaking Truth with Love	133
Chapter 30	Creativity: Unlocking Human Potential	137
Chapter 31	Presence: The Power of Now	140
Chapter 32	Resilience: Bounding Forward, Not Just Back	143
Chapter 33	Humility: The Strength of Being Grounded	146
Chapter 34	Vision: Seeing Beyond the Present	149
Chapter 35	Unity Beyond the Self	152

Part VI: The Circle of Transformation — **155**

| Chapter 36 | The Circle of Transformation | 156 |

Part I: The Call to Greatness

Chapter 1—What Makes The Very Best

The Story: The Young Violinist

It begins in a small concert hall, where a teenage violinist, hands trembling, takes her seat. The world doesn't yet know her name, she isn't the most technically advanced musician in her class, and she isn't from a famous family. Yet when she plays, something unusual happens: the room grows still, the air thickens with attention; and people are moved, not just by her accuracy, but by her presence, by the way her music feels like it is reaching into their own stories.

As she plays, an older man in the audience whispers, 'This girl will be remembered.'

Why? She wasn't the fastest, the loudest, or flawless. However, she was unmistakably herself, and she carried a depth that only comes from discipline, vision, and something more—a quality that makes the very best rise above the rest.

Conversation: Mardoche and Karen

Mardoche: Karen, I've often wondered—what is it that makes someone the best? Not just good, not just excellent, but the kind of person who leaves an imprint.

Karen: You mean the ones we write about in history books, or the ones whose names come to us when we think of mastery—Freud, Mandela, Serena, Maya Angelou?

Mardoche: Exactly. We celebrate them, but if you peel back the myth, what's behind it?

Karen: Science tells us it isn't raw talent alone. It's about what we call in psychology, deliberate practice. Anders Ericsson's research showed that greatness comes from stretching yourself at the edge of your abilities, day after day, not from playing it safe.

Mardoche: Right. That's the conscious level of our model: Discipline, Habits, Daily choices. Yer, that's not enough. I've met many who worked hard but never became extraordinary.

Karen: That's because the preconscious level matters too: the patterns and schemas underneath. If someone believes deep down, 'I don't deserve to shine,' that will sabotage even the best training.

Mardoche: And the unconscious layer, which is what we bury and repress. That's where defenses like rationalization or projection live. Until people do the work of free association, dream analysis, free association journaling, and deep therapy, those forces run the show.

Karen: Which leads us to the existential layer: choosing meaning. You can master skills, heal old wounds, and shift beliefs; but if you don't decide what your life stands for, you'll never step into recognition. The very best aren't just skilled; rather, they're anchored in purpose.

Science of Being the Best

Research across psychology, neuroscience, and leadership studies points to eight recurring traits that separate the best from the rest:

1. Deliberate Practice – Ericsson (2006) showed that expertise is built by focused, feedback-driven practice.
2. Grit – Duckworth (2016) proved passion and perseverance matter more than IQ or talent.
3. Flow – Csikszentmihalyi (1990) demonstrated peak performance arises in flow states.
4. Resilience – Neuroscience reveals how the brain rewires through adversity (Southwick & Charney, 2012).
5. Uniqueness – Recognition comes from originality (Simonton, 2011).
6. Emotional Intelligence – Goleman (1995) showed connection predicts leadership success.
7. Consistency – Habits and rituals wire identity (Clear, 2018).

8. Purpose Beyond Self – Frankl (1946) showed meaning is the deepest driver of excellence.

Toolbox: Your First Steps Toward Greatness

1. Reflection Prompt: Think of someone you admire. What specifically makes them unforgettable?
2. Inquiry Exercise: What is your unique signature—the thing only you can bring?
3. Commitment Practice: Choose one daily habit. Commit to practicing it for 30 days, tracking it daily.

Integration with the 4 Layers of Transformation

- Conscious Layer: Begin with behavior—new routines, disciplined practice.
- Preconscious Layer: Notice limiting beliefs and schemas; challenge them.
- Unconscious Layer: Journal dreams, explore defenses, bring hidden material into awareness.
- Existential Layer: Ask, 'What does being the best mean for me, for my life, for my service to others?'

Closing Narrative

The young violinist bows at the end of her performance. She is not yet world-famous, but she has begun the path: discipline, resilience, uniqueness, and purpose. She may stumble, fail, or be forgotten for a time; but if she keeps moving through the four layers, she will become more than a musician, she will become unforgettable.

And so can we.

References

- Csikszentmihalyi, M. (1990). Flow: The Psychology of Optimal Experience. Harper & Row.
- Duckworth, A. (2016). Grit: The Power of Passion and Perseverance. Scribner.
- Ericsson, K. A., et al. (2006). The Cambridge Handbook of Expertise and Expert Performance. Cambridge University Press.
- Frankl, V. E. (1946). Man's Search for Meaning. Beacon Press.
- Goleman, D. (1995). Emotional Intelligence. Bantam Books.
- Simonton, D. K. (2011). Creativity and recognition. Review of General Psychology, 15(2), 158–174.
- Southwick, S. M., & Charney, D. S. (2012). Resilience: The Science of Mastering Life's Greatest Challenges. Cambridge University Press.
- Clear, J. (2018). Atomic Habits. Avery.

Chapter 2—The Myths of Talent and Luck

The Story: The Runner Nobody Saw Coming

At a dusty track in a small town, the crowd gathers to watch the national finals. All eyes are on the star, an athlete everyone calls a 'natural.' His stride is effortless, his muscles seemingly built for speed. However, when the starting gun cracks, something surprising happens.

Another runner, shorter, less celebrated, and with no magazine features or sponsors, pushes forward. He doesn't win on the first burst, but lap by lap, he closes in. On the final stretch, it's not the 'natural' who breaks the tape, but the underdog who trained through rain, ice, and exhaustion, unseen by the cameras.

Later, the newspapers call him 'lucky.' But was it luck? or something else?

Conversation: Mardoche and Karen

Mardoche: Karen, don't you think people love to explain away greatness with words like talent and luck?

Karen: Absolutely. It's comforting. If someone is simply 'gifted,' then the rest of us are excused from trying.

Mardoche: But the truth is, talent alone is never enough. How many 'naturals' have we seen who never fulfilled their promise?

Karen: Exactly. Studies in expertise show that early ability only explains a fraction of long-term success. And luck? Of course circumstances matter, but what looks like luck is often preparation meeting opportunity.

Mardoche: Which is why we need to debunk the myths. Otherwise, people stay trapped in excuses instead of transformation.

Karen: And here's where our 4-layer model comes in:

- Conscious level: the so-called 'lucky break' is useless if someone hasn't built habits and discipline.
- Preconscious level: if someone believes success depends on fate, they won't persist.
- Unconscious level: fear of failure or repressed shame can block talent from surfacing.
- Existential level: greatness comes when people stop waiting for luck and choose responsibility for their meaning.

Science of the Myths

1. Talent Is Overrated – Research by Ericsson & Pool (2016) shows mastery depends on deliberate practice, not innate genius.
2. Luck Favors the Prepared – Richard Wiseman (2003) found that 'lucky people' are open, persistent, and resilient.
3. Growth Mindset – Carol Dweck (2006) proved that believing ability can grow leads to greater outcomes.
4. Survivorship Bias – We glorify winners we see, forgetting those who had similar talent but lacked persistence.

Case Studies

- Mozart: Often called a prodigy, but trained rigorously by his father.
- Oprah Winfrey: Fired early in her career, turned setbacks into fuel.
- Michael Jordan: Cut from his high school team, practiced relentlessly and became the greatest.

Toolbox: Reframing Talent and Luck

1. Reflection Prompt: Recall a time you dismissed someone as 'lucky' or 'gifted.' What effort did you overlook?

2. Inquiry Exercise: What beliefs do you carry about talent and luck? Do they empower or excuse you?
3. Commitment Practice: Choose one skill you think you 'lack talent for.' Practice 20 minutes daily for a week.

Integration with the 4 Layers of Transformation

- Conscious Layer: Build deliberate habits—don't wait for luck.
- Preconscious Layer: Rewrite schemas: 'I wasn't born with it' → 'I can build it.'
- Unconscious Layer: Explore hidden fears or shame that block effort.
- Existential Layer: Accept radical responsibility—life is not a lottery, it's a canvas.

Closing Narrative

The runner who crossed the finish line that day wasn't chosen by fortune. He was chosen by his sweat, persistence, and refusal to let talent or luck define him.

When people called him 'lucky,' he smiled. Because he knew greatness is not a gift; rather, a decision, renewed daily.

And that decision is open to all of us.

References

- Dweck, C. (2006). Mindset: The New Psychology of Success. Random House.
- Ericsson, A., & Pool, R. (2016). Peak: Secrets from the New Science of Expertise. Houghton Mifflin Harcourt.
- Jordan, M. (1994). I Can't Accept Not Trying: Michael Jordan on the Pursuit of Excellence. Harper San Francisco.
- Wiseman, R. (2003). The Luck Factor: The Scientific Study of the Lucky Mind. Miramax Books.

Part II: The Four Layers of Transformation

Chapter 3—Conscious Layer: Discipline and Daily Practice

The Story: The Dancer's Dawn

Every morning before the city awoke, a dancer tied her shoes and stepped into an empty studio. There are no cameras and there is no applause; rather, just the rhythm of her own breath against silence.

She wasn't the most talented in her company, and in fact, others could leap higher, or turn sharper; yet day after day, she arrived before dawn, drilling the same movements, refining details no one else would notice.

Years later, when her name was whispered with reverence, people said, 'She was born for this.' But she knew the truth: she was not born; she was built, one dawn at a time.

Conversation: Mardoche and Karen

Karen: Discipline gets such a bad reputation. People hear the word and think of rigidity, punishment, or lack of freedom.

Mardoche: Yet discipline is the root of freedom. At the conscious level, it's the practices, the routines, and the choices that wire greatness into daily life.

Karen: Exactly, and without it, even talent goes nowhere. Without it, it's like having seeds but never planting them.

Mardoche: And it's not about perfection, it's about showing up. Neuroscience tells us habits carve pathways into the brain, consistency creates identity.

Karen: That's why at the conscious layer, transformation begins with the basics: sleep, nutrition, exercise, stress management, meditation, breath awareness. They're the foundations of the extraordinary.

Mardoche: You need to manage the conscious level to have the strength to face the deeper layers.

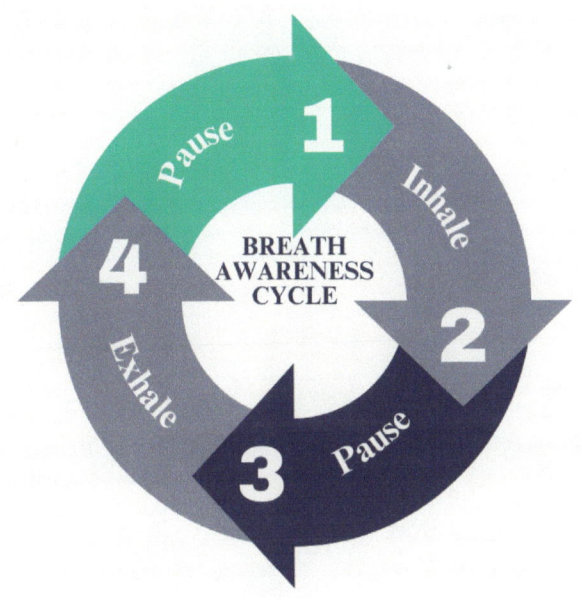

Science of Discipline and Daily Practice

1. Neuroplasticity and Habits – Habits create neural pathways (Doidge, 2007). Repeated behaviors strengthen synaptic connections.
2. Sleep and Performance – Sleep improves memory consolidation, focus, and creativity (Walker, 2017).
3. Exercise and Cognition – Physical activity boosts neurogenesis and resilience (Ratey, 2008
4. Mindfulness and Self-Regulation – Meditation rewires the brain (Tang et al., 2015).
5. The Power of Small Wins – Tiny changes compound into remarkable results (Clear, 2018).

Mindfulness Stop Tool

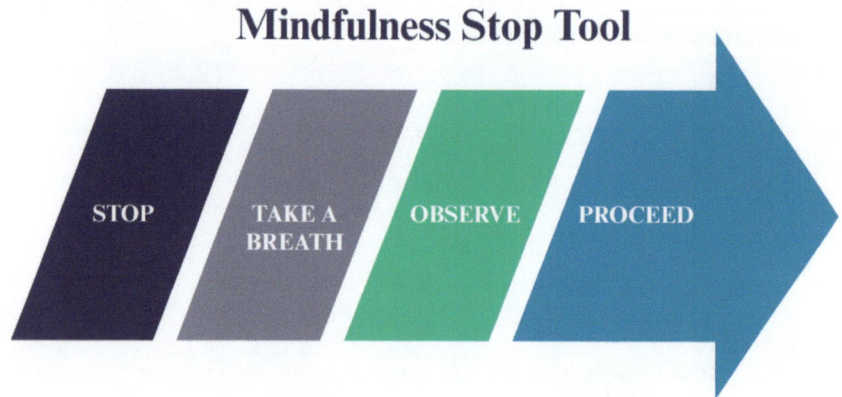

Case Studies
- Kobe Bryant: Known for his '4 a.m. workouts,' believing discipline created separation
- Maya Angelou: Wrote every day in a rented hotel room, turning routine into art.
- Benjamin Franklin: Used structured daily schedules harmonizing work, rest, and reflection.

Toolbox: Daily Practice Builder
1. Reflection Prompt: What one daily practice already strengthens you? How could you deepen it?
2. Inquiry Exercise: Which daily habits currently drain your energy or focus? List them.
3. Commitment Practice: Choose one 'anchor habit' (e.g., 20 minutes meditation, journaling, exercise). Commit for 30 days.

Integration with the 4 Layers of Transformation
- Conscious Layer: Create structure: habits, health, routines.
- Preconscious Layer: Notice beliefs about discipline (e.g., 'It's too hard' → 'Every practice makes me stronger').
- Unconscious Layer: Explore resistances to discipline (self-sabotage, procrastination).

- Existential Layer: Remember why you practice: for freedom, meaning, and purpose.

Closing Narrative

The dancer's dawns were not glamorous; but discipline made her body a vessel for art.

Years later, when the spotlight found her, people called her 'gifted.'

But she smiled, remembering the mornings no one saw.

The conscious layer had carried her to greatness.

And it can carry us, too.

References

- Clear, J. (2018). Atomic Habits. Avery.
- Doidge, N. (2007). The Brain That Changes Itself. Viking.
- Franklin, B. (1791). Autobiography of Benjamin Franklin. Philadelphia.
- Ratey, J. (2008). Spark: The Revolutionary New Science of Exercise and the Brain. Little, Brown.
- Tang, Y. Y., et al. (2015). The neuroscience of mindfulness meditation. Nature Reviews Neuroscience, 16(4), 213–225.
- Walker, M. (2017). Why We Sleep. Scribner.

Chapter 4—Preconscious Layer: Schemas and Patterns

The Story: The Teacher's Shadow

Maria was a gifted teacher. Her students loved her energy, her creativity, her care; while every year, when she was nominated for an award, she quietly withdrew her application. 'I'm not that kind of person,' she would say.

Where did this belief come from? In childhood, she had been told not to 'show off.' The message took root: standing out is dangerous. Though she had long forgotten those exact words, the pattern remained, operating just below awareness, at the preconscious level.

It wasn't until therapy, years later, that Maria realized she had been living in the shadow of a schema, a hidden script dictating her choices. Once she named it, she was free to choose differently.

Conversation: Mardoche and Karen

Mardoche: The preconscious is fascinating; and while it's not buried as deeply as the unconscious, it's rather powerful.

Karen: Exactly. It's like the operating system running in the background. We don't always notice it, yet it shapes everything, including our decisions, our relationships, and even our sense of possibility.

Mardoche: And schemas, those mental frameworks we build early on, become the invisible architects of our lives.

Karen: This is so, unless we pause to notice them. Schema Therapy, for example, helps people identify these patterns and challenge them.

Mardoche: At the preconscious level, transformation means surfacing these 'default settings,' and examining whether they still serve us, and rewriting them.

Emotion Regulation Toolkit

| Grounding | Reframing | Expression | Connection |

Science of Schemas and Patterns
1. Schemas Defined – Young's Schema Therapy (2003) describes schemas as enduring, self-defeating themes.
2. Attachment and Beliefs – Bowlby and Ainsworth showed how early relationships shape beliefs.
3. Mindfulness and Pattern Awareness – Mindfulness helps bring implicit beliefs into awareness (Shapiro et al., 2006).
4. ACT and Cognitive Defusion – ACT helps people observe thoughts without being fused to them (Hayes et al., 2012).
5. Gestalt Therapy – Emphasizes awareness of 'unfinished business' carried forward until acknowledged.

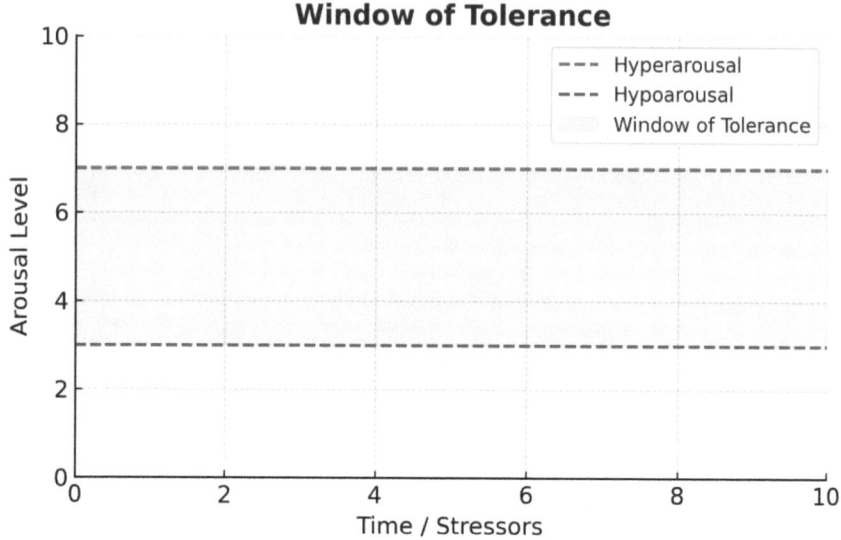

Case Studies

- The Perfectionist: Raised with conditional love, later avoids risk to maintain approval.
- The Abandoned Child: Overcompensates by clinging in adult relationships.
- The Self-Sacrificer: Taught early that their needs don't matter, later burns out by always giving.

Toolbox: Uncovering Your Schemas

1. Reflection Prompt: What recurring theme shows up in your relationships, career, or self-talk?
2. Inquiry Exercise: Ask, 'Whose voice is this belief? Is it mine— or something I inherited?'
3. Commitment Practice: For the next week, notice one repeated pattern. Pause, name it, and ask: 'What new choice is possible?'

Integration with the 4 Layers of Transformation

- Conscious Layer: Keep daily habits that support awareness (journaling, meditation).

- Preconscious Layer: Identify, challenge, and rewrite schemas.
- Unconscious Layer: Explore deeper defenses that reinforce schemas.
- Existential Layer: Choose meaning beyond inherited scripts.

Closing Narrative

Maria finally submitted her award application. She didn't win that year, but she no longer lived under the old story. Each choice afterward felt freer, truer.

The preconscious layer had shifted; and when patterns shift, lives transform.

References

- Ainsworth, M. D. S., & Bowlby, J. (1991). An ethological approach to personality development. American Psychologist, 46(4), 333–341.
- Hayes, S. C., Strosahl, K. D., & Wilson, K. G. (2012). Acceptance and Commitment Therapy. Guilford Press.
- Shapiro, S. L., et al. (2006). Mechanisms of mindfulness. Journal of Clinical Psychology, 62(3), 373–386.
- Young, J. E., Klosko, J. S., & Weishaar, M. E. (2003). Schema Therapy: A Practitioner's Guide. Guilford Press.
- Perls, F. (1969). Gestalt Therapy Verbatim. Real People Press.

Chapter 5—Unconscious Layer: The Hidden Self

The Story: The Dream That Wouldn't Go Away

David kept dreaming of a locked room. Every night, the same hallway, the same door. He never opened it, he never knew what was inside.

In his waking life, David was successful, respected, even admired. However, something gnawed at him, something like a vague dissatisfaction, like a shadow of unease.

One day in therapy, the dream returned; and his therapist asked, *'What do you imagine might be behind the door?'*

David hesitated, his chest tightened, tears welled, and slowly, he whispered: *'My father's voice... telling me I'll never be enough.'*

The unconscious had spoken, and what had been buried was not gone; rather, it was alive, shaping his choices, his relationships, and his very sense of self.

Conversation: Mardoche and Karen

Karen: The unconscious is like a storage room for everything we can't face. Memories, fears, desires, don't disappear; rather, they just go underground.

Mardoche: And when they're underground, they drive us. Freud called it the 'return of the repressed.' What we push away comes back, through dreams, slips of the tongue, and projections.

Karen: Which is why the unconscious layer is essential for transformation. Without it, people can change behaviors and even beliefs, but they'll keep repeating patterns they don't understand.

Mardoche: Exactly. That's why psychodynamic psychotherapy or psychoanalysis uses tools like free association, dream analysis, transference, and interpretation. They bring the hidden self into the light.

Karen: And once people confront what was hidden, they don't just understand themselves, they also reclaim their freedom.

Science of the Unconscious

1. Repression and Defenses – Vaillant (1992) categorized defenses from immature to mature; repression and denial protect short-term but sabotage long-term.
2. Dreams as Windows – Freud (1900) called dreams 'the royal road to the unconscious.' Modern neuroscience shows dreams integrate memory and emotion.
3. Projection and Transference – Psychoanalysis shows how people disown unacceptable feelings, projecting them onto others.
4. Free Association – Narrative therapy and expressive writing reduce symptoms by integrating memory (Pennebaker & Smyth, 2016).
5. Working Through – Transformation requires not just insight but repeated confrontation and integration of unconscious material.

Brain and Mind Layers

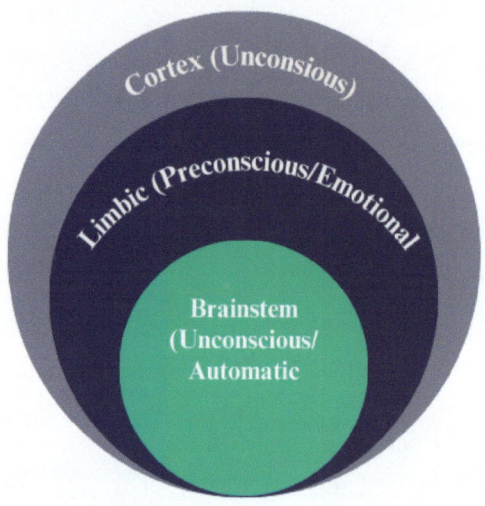

Case Studies

- The Angry Boss: Projects his own insecurity onto employees.
- The Withdrawn Partner: Avoids intimacy due to repressed abandonment fears.
- The Overachiever: Driven by buried shame of childhood criticism.

Toolbox: Meeting the Hidden Self

1. Reflection Prompt: Recall your last dream. What feelings did it stir? What could those symbolize?
2. Inquiry Exercise: Notice projections: Who frustrates you most? What part of yourself are you seeing in them?
3. Commitment Practice: Keep a daily 'unconscious journal.' Write freely for 10 minutes without censoring. Review weekly.

Integration with the 4 Layers of Transformation
- Conscious Layer: Track behaviors and emotions.
- Preconscious Layer: Identify patterns and schemas.
- Unconscious Layer: Explore repressed material with journaling, therapy, or dream analysis.
- Existential Layer: Transform pain into meaning, integrating all layers into freedom and choice.

Closing Narrative

David never stopped dreaming, but over time, the door opened. Inside, he found grief, rage, and shame, but also tenderness.

By facing the hidden self, he discovered he was not condemned by the past. He realized he could choose differently, he could live freely.

And this is the gift of the unconscious: when the hidden becomes known, the prisoner becomes free.

References
- Freud, S. (1900). The Interpretation of Dreams. Basic Books.
- Pennebaker, J. W., & Smyth, J. M. (2016). Opening Up by Writing It Down. Guilford Press.
- Vaillant, G. (1992). Ego Mechanisms of Defense: A Guide for Clinicians and Researchers. American Psychiatric Press.
- Jung, C. G. (1964). Man and His Symbols. Doubleday.
- Westen, D. (1998). The scientific status of unconscious processes. Annual Review of Psychology, 49, 521–549.

Chapter 6— Existential Layer: Freedom, Meaning, and Integration

The Story: The Prisoner Who Found Meaning

In a concentration camp during World War II, Viktor Frankl faced unspeakable suffering. Stripped of possessions, dignity, and freedom, he saw many prisoners wither into despair. Yet Frankl observed something remarkable: those who found meaning, even in suffering, were more likely to endure.

Frankl himself survived, not because he was stronger or luckier, but because he discovered a reason to live: the possibility of helping others by teaching them that even in suffering, life holds meaning. Out of the ashes of atrocity, he wrote Man's Search for Meaning, one of the most influential books of the 20th century.

The existential layer is where transformation becomes whole. It is where freedom is claimed, meaning is chosen, and integration becomes life itself.

Conversation: Mardoche and Karen

Mardoche: The conscious, preconscious, and unconscious layers prepare the ground. However, the existential layer, that's where we ask: 'What does my life stand for?'

Karen: Exactly. Without this layer, people might change behaviors, reframe beliefs, even uncover unconscious drives, but they can still feel empty.

Mardoche: Because meaning isn't given; rather, it's chosen. Kierkegaard, Sartre, Frankl, they all said the same thing: freedom is responsibility.

Karen: And integration means taking everything, our habits, our patterns, our unconscious material, and choosing how we will live with them; and, not in denial, not in repression, but in freedom.

Mardoche: Which is why the existential layer is not about erasing the past; rather, it's about using it as raw material for purpose.

Science of Freedom and Meaning

1. Logotherapy (Frankl, 1946) – Meaning is the strongest motivator of human life.
2. Existential Psychology (Yalom, 1980) – Facing death, freedom, isolation, and meaninglessness leads to authentic living.
3. Self-Determination Theory (Deci & Ryan, 1985) – Autonomy, competence, and relatedness foster chosen meaning.
4. Positive Psychology (Seligman, 2011) – Living with meaning is essential for wellbeing.
5. The Golden Rule and Ethics – Reciprocity and ethics are universal pillars of meaning (Roes & Raymond, 2003).

Case Studies

- Nelson Mandela: Turned imprisonment into a platform for reconciliation.
- Malala Yousafzai: Transformed trauma into advocacy for education.
- Everyday Heroes: People who turn hardship into service or community building.

Toolbox: Choosing Meaning

1. Reflection Prompt: What is one hardship you've faced? What meaning can you draw from it?
2. Inquiry Exercise: Write your own 'meaning statement': 'My life stands for…'

3. Commitment Practice: Each morning, identify one action that reflects your chosen purpose.

Integration with the 4 Layers of Transformation

- Conscious Layer: Live with structure and discipline.
- Preconscious Layer: Rewrite patterns and schemas.
- Unconscious Layer: Face hidden material.
- Existential Layer: Integrate all into freedom and chosen meaning.

Closing Narrative

In Man's Search for Meaning, Frankl wrote, 'Those who have a why to live can bear almost any how.'

The existential layer is where transformation ripens into wholeness. It is where we stop asking, *'What happened to me?'* and begin asking, *'What will I make of it?'*

Here, the past is not erased; rather, it is integrated; and in that integration, freedom begins.

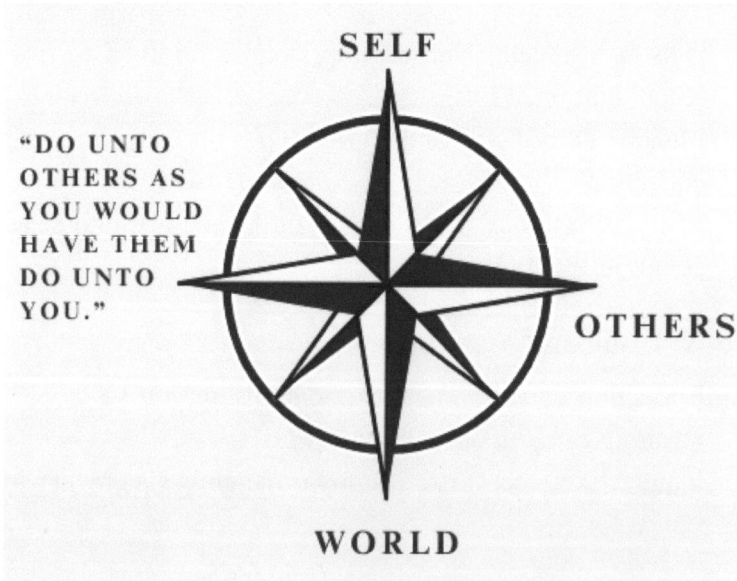

References

- Deci, E. L., & Ryan, R. M. (1985). Intrinsic Motivation and Self-Determination in Human Behavior. Springer.
- Frankl, V. E. (1946). Man's Search for Meaning. Beacon Press.
- Roes, F. L., & Raymond, M. (2003). Reciprocity and ethics across cultures. Behavioral and Brain Sciences, 26(5), 593–607.
- Seligman, M. E. P. (2011). Flourish. Free Press.
- Yalom, I. D. (1980). Existential Psychotherapy. Basic Books.

ICEBERG MODEL OF THE MIND

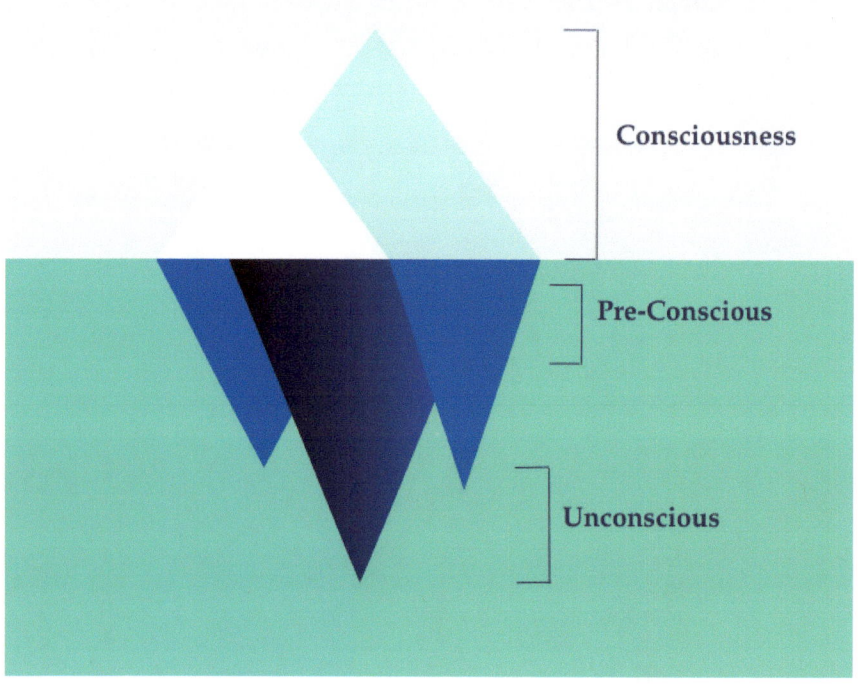

Part III: Becoming Recognized

Chapter 7—Uniqueness: Your Irreplaceable Signature

The Story: The Painter Who Refused to Copy

Amara grew up studying the great masters of art; and her teachers encouraged her to imitate their techniques, and replicate their brushstrokes. She became very skilled, but she felt invisible.

One night, restless and unsatisfied, she painted not what she was taught but what she felt. The colors clashed, the forms broke convention, and she almost threw it away. Instead, she showed it to a friend who gasped, 'This is you. No one else could have painted this.'

What ensued was nothing short of a miracle. Amara's career began the moment she stopped trying to be the best copy, and started being the only original.

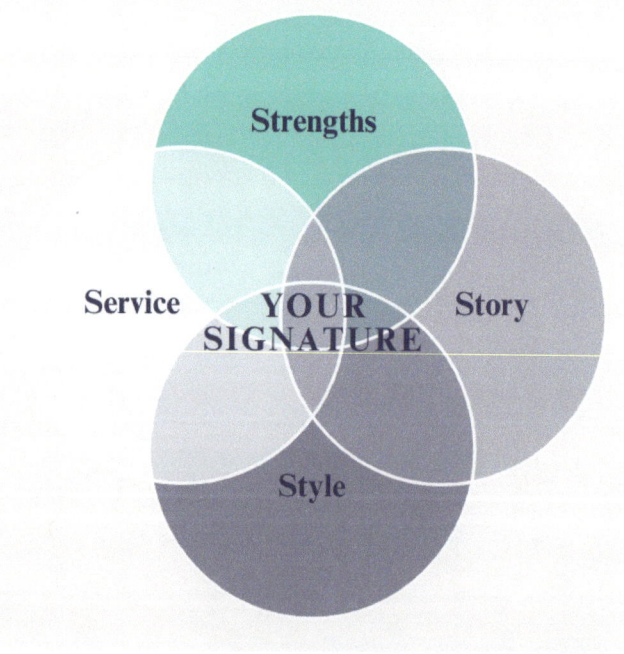

Conversation: Mardoche and Karen

Karen: We admire excellence, but what we remember is uniqueness.

Mardoche: Right. Plenty of people are skilled, but only a few carry a signature so unmistakable that we say, 'That was theirs.'

Karen: And uniqueness isn't just creativity, it's also authenticity. It's integrating all layers of the self and bringing forth something no one else can.

Mardoche: Which is why comparison is deadly. If you're measuring yourself by others, you're not discovering your own voice.

Karen: Exactly. At the conscious level, uniqueness shows in habits of experimentation. At the preconscious level, it's breaking free from limiting schemas that say 'fit in.' At the unconscious level, it's reclaiming repressed parts of the self. And at the existential layer, it's declaring, 'This is who I choose to be.'

Science of Uniqueness

1. Originality and Creativity – Adam Grant (2016) found creative leaders weren't the most gifted but the most willing to risk and express their perspective.
2. Authenticity and Wellbeing – Authenticity correlates with higher life satisfaction and lower stress (Kernis & Goldman, 2006).
3. Neuroscience of Creativity – Research shows creativity arises from integration of divergent and convergent thinking (Beaty et al., 2016).
4. Identity and Distinction – Erikson's theory highlights identity as a lifelong task; uniqueness is part of maturity.

Case Studies
- Steve Jobs: Fused design, art, and function in unprecedented ways.
- Frida Kahlo: Turned pain and disability into an unmistakable artistic voice.
- Maya Angelou: Blended poetry, autobiography, and advocacy into a singular form.

Toolbox: Discovering Your Signature
1. Reflection Prompt: What do people consistently say only you bring to the table?
2. Inquiry Exercise: If you weren't afraid of judgment, what would you create, say, or do differently?
3. Commitment Practice: Choose one way this week to express your uniqueness, whether in work, relationships, or art.

Integration with the 4 Layers of Transformation
- Conscious Layer: Experiment with daily practices that allow individuality to emerge.
- Preconscious Layer: Challenge inherited schemas that say 'don't stand out.'
- Unconscious Layer: Reclaim hidden or suppressed aspects of self-expression.
- Existential Layer: Choose to live authentically, turning uniqueness into contribution.

Closing Narrative

When Amara first painted like herself, it frightened her. But soon, that painting became the one everyone remembered.

She discovered what the very best know: skill earns respect, but uniqueness earns immortality.

And your irreplaceable signature is waiting too—not in imitation, but in the courage to be fully you.

References

- Beaty, R. E., et al. (2016). Creativity and the brain's default mode network. NeuroImage, 129, 346–354.
- Erikson, E. H. (1959). Identity and the Life Cycle. International Universities Press.
- Grant, A. (2016). Originals: How Non-Conformists Move the World. Viking.
- Kernis, M. H., & Goldman, B. M. (2006). Authenticity as a psychological construct. Review of General Psychology, 10(1), 93–126.

Chapter 8—Consistency: Excellence as a Lifestyle

The Story: The Marathoner's Secret

When asked how he managed to finish 50 marathons in 50 days, the runner smiled and said, *'I never ran 50 marathons. I ran one marathon — 50 times.'*

People expected a secret hack. They wanted to hear about supplements, gear, or natural gifts. Instead, his answer revealed the truth: greatness is not in what you do once, but in what you do every day.

Consistency is the secret ingredient of excellence. It is not glamorous, it is not flashy; rather, it is steady, reliable, and relentless.

Conversation: Mardoche and Karen

Karen: Consistency is underrated. People chase motivation, but motivation is fickle. Consistency is what builds legacies.

Mardoche: Yes. The best don't rely on moods; rather, they rely on systems. They don't ask, 'Do I feel like it today?' Rather, they ask, 'What is my commitment?'

Karen: Exactly. At the conscious level, consistency is daily rituals. At the preconscious level, it's reshaping the belief that progress requires perfection. At the unconscious level, it's exposing the defenses that make consistency a battle. And at the existential layer, it's about embodying excellence as a way of being, not just doing.

Mardoche: Which is why the consistent aren't remembered for one great act, but for a life of steady contribution.

Science of Consistency
1. Habit Formation – Habits automate excellence. Repeated behaviors create identity-shaping routines (Clear, 2018).
2. Compound Effect – Small actions, compounded over time, yield massive results (Hardy, 2010).
3. Neuroscience of Repetition – Dopamine reinforcement loops wire behaviors into automatic circuits (Schultz, 2016).
4. Self-Discipline and Grit – Duckworth (2016) showed consistency of effort predicts success more than talent.
5. Reliability and Trust – Leadership research finds consistency builds credibility more than charisma (Kouzes & Posner, 2017).

Consistency: Habit Loop

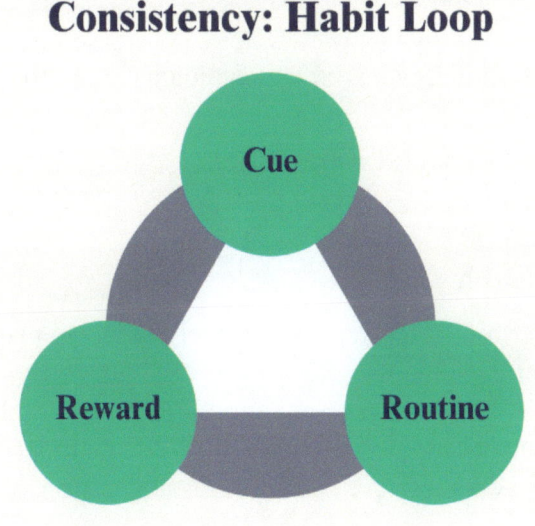

Case Studies
- Serena Williams: Decades of disciplined training created dominance and longevity.
- Mahatma Gandhi: Consistent nonviolence became more powerful than any single act.

- Daily Writers: From Stephen King to Maya Angelou, consistency turned pages into masterpieces.

Toolbox: Building a Lifestyle of Consistency

1. Reflection Prompt: Where in your life have you been expressing consistency—and what has it given you?
2. Inquiry Exercise: Identify one area where inconsistency holds you back. What defense or belief sustains it?
3. Commitment Practice: Choose a 'non-negotiable' habit. Practice it daily for 30 days without exception.

Integration with the 4 Layers of Transformation

- Conscious Layer: Ritualize excellence through daily habits.
- Preconscious Layer: Challenge perfectionism—progress, not perfection, builds consistency.
- Unconscious Layer: Expose avoidance and procrastination as defenses.
- Existential Layer: Live consistency as a way of being, aligning habits with chosen values.

Closing Narrative

The marathoner didn't master a secret technique. He mastered the art of showing up—again and again.

Excellence is not an act; rather, it is a lifestyle; and when consistency becomes your compass, greatness is not a question of if—only of when.

References

- Clear, J. (2018). Atomic Habits. Avery.
- Duckworth, A. (2016). Grit: The Power of Passion and Perseverance. Scribner.
- Hardy, D. (2010). The Compound Effect. Vanguard Press.
- Kouzes, J. M., & Posner, B. Z. (2017). The Leadership Challenge. Wiley.
- Schultz, W. (2016). Dopamine reward prediction error coding. Handbook of Behavioral Neuroscience, 27, 199–213.

Chapter 9—Connection: The Human Element

The Story: The Doctor Who Remembered a Name

A world-renowned physician was once asked what made patients love him so much. His treatments were excellent, but so were those of his colleagues. He smiled and said, *'I remember their names, I hold their hands, and I listen.'*

Years later, a patient who survived a terrifying illness told reporters: *'The medicine saved me, but his presence healed me.'*

Connection is the difference between competence and greatness. It is the invisible thread that turns skill into impact, knowledge into wisdom, and action into legacy.

Conversation: Mardoche and Karen

Karen: Connection is the element we sometimes forget when we talk about being 'the best.' People assume it's all about talent or results.

Mardoche: Yet people rarely remember what you did. They remember how you made them feel.

Karen: Exactly. Emotional intelligence, empathy, presence—these are what make excellence human.

Mardoche: And it's not soft or secondary. Connection improves outcomes, whether in healthcare, therapy, leadership, education, or wherever humans are involved, connection multiplies effectiveness.

Karen: At the conscious level, connection looks like active listening. At the preconscious level, it's challenging the schemas that keep us guarded. At the unconscious level, it's facing the projections and defenses that block intimacy. And at the existential level, it's choosing to see the humanity in every encounter.

Science of Connection

1. Emotional Intelligence (Goleman, 1995) – Predicts leadership success more strongly than IQ or technical skill.
2. Empathy and Healing – Empathy in healthcare improves adherence, satisfaction, and outcomes (Hojat, 2007).
3. Mirror Neurons – Neuroscience shows our brains are wired for resonance; connection is biological (Rizzolatti & Craighero, 2004).
4. Therapeutic Alliance – Alliance predicts outcomes more than the specific technique (Wampold, 2015).
5. Belonging and Performance – Social connection improves motivation, resilience, and longevity (Holt-Lunstad, 2010).

Case Studies

- Barack Obama: Inspired not only through words but through resonance with dignity.
- Mother Teresa: Saw and touched the forgotten, embodying radical presence.
- Everyday Teachers, Leaders, Clinicians: Remembered not for brilliance, but for connection.

Toolbox: Strengthening Connection

1. Reflection Prompt: Who in your life makes you feel most seen? What do they do that creates that feeling?
2. Inquiry Exercise: In your last three conversations, were you more focused on responding or listening?
3. Commitment Practice: Choose one person today and practice presence: eye contact, silence, listening without interruption.

Validation Ladder

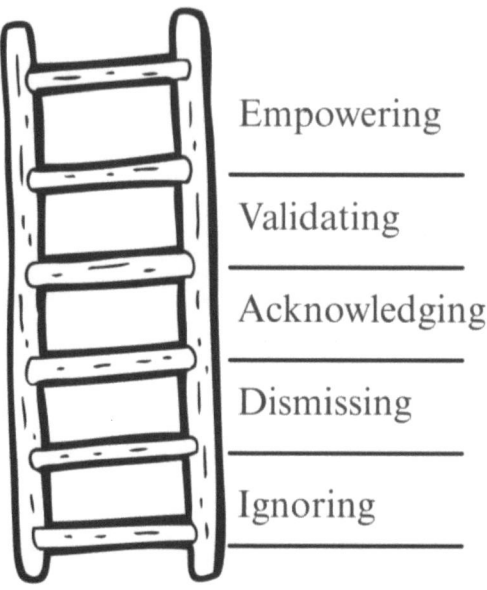

Integration with the 4 Layers of Transformation

- Conscious Layer: Practice listening, remembering names, eye contact.
- Preconscious Layer: Challenge beliefs like 'connection is weakness.'
- Unconscious Layer: Face defenses that avoid vulnerability.
- Existential Layer: Choose to live as if every human interaction matters—because it does.

Closing Narrative

The doctor's greatest medicine wasn't in a bottle—it was in his eyes, his voice, his touch.

Connection transforms the ordinary into the extraordinary. It is the human element that ensures excellence is not just admired but felt.

And in the end, to be the best is not to stand above others, but to stand with them.

References

- Goleman, D. (1995). Emotional Intelligence. Bantam Books.
- Hojat, M. (2007). Empathy in Patient Care. Springer.
- Holt-Lunstad, J., et al. (2010). Social relationships and mortality risk. PLoS Medicine, 7(7), e1000316.
- Rizzolatti, G., & Craighero, L. (2004). Mirror neuron system. Annual Review of Neuroscience, 27, 169–192.
- Wampold, B. E. (2015). How important are common factors in psychotherapy? World Psychiatry, 14(3), 270–277.

Chapter 10: Resilience and Reinvention

The Story: The Musician Who Played Again

When a car accident shattered his hand, Miguel, a professional pianist, was told he would never play again. For months, he spiraled into despair for his identity had been tied to his music.

One day, in rehab, his therapist asked, *'What else in you can still make music?'*

Miguel then began composing with software, teaching others, and even conducting. Eventually, with adapted technique, he returned to the piano, differently, but powerfully.

He hadn't just survived. He had reinvented himself.

Conversation: Mardoche and Karen

Mardoche: Resilience isn't just bouncing back; rather, it's bouncing forward.

Karen: Exactly. Some people think resilience means ignoring pain. But true resilience acknowledges loss, then transforms it.

Mardoche: And reinvention is resilience at its highest form. It's not about returning to the old, but creating something new.

Karen: At the conscious layer, resilience is habits that regulate stress. At the preconscious layer, it's changing beliefs like 'I can't go on.' At the unconscious layer, it's facing the grief and fear we repress. And at the existential layer, it's choosing to define hardship as a path to growth.

Mardoche: Which is why the very best aren't those who never fall; rather, they're those who fall and rise transformed.

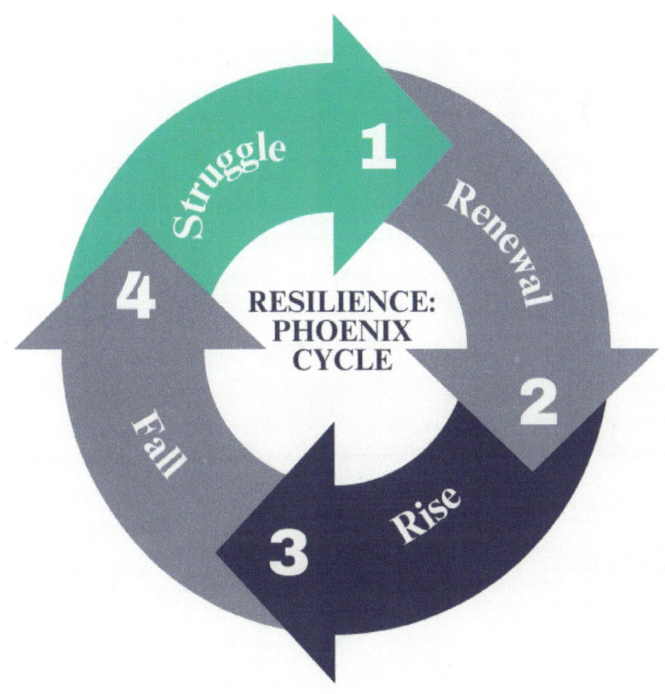

Science of Resilience and Reinvention

1. Post-Traumatic Growth (Tedeschi & Calhoun, 1996) – Trauma can lead to greater appreciation of life and new possibilities.
2. Stress Inoculation (Meichenbaum, 2007) – Training to face manageable stressors builds long-term resilience.
3. Neuroplasticity (Doidge, 2007) – The brain rewires after injury and adversity, supporting reinvention.
4. Growth Mindset (Dweck, 2006) – Belief in the ability to grow fuels resilience and adaptability.
5. Meaning-Making and Recovery – People who find meaning in hardship recover more fully and with greater satisfaction (Park, 2010).

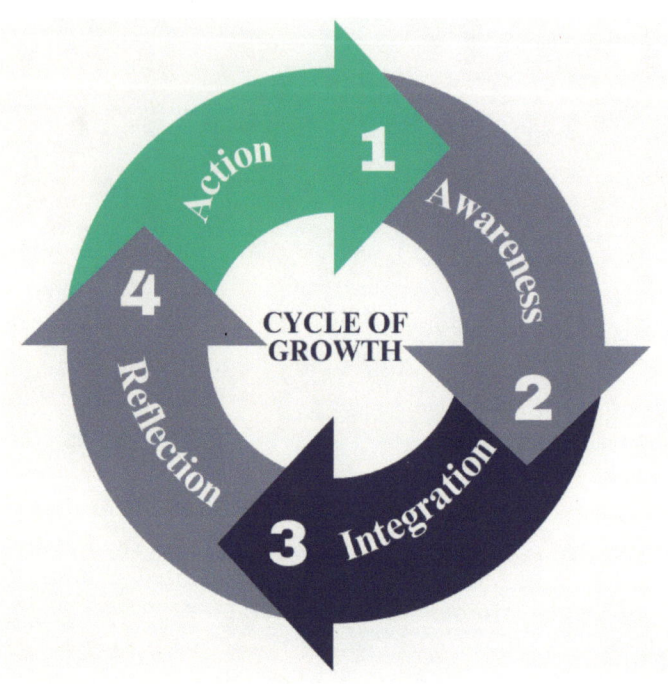

Case Studies

- Oprah Winfrey: Transformed a traumatic childhood into a platform for empowerment.
- Nelson Mandela: Turned 27 years in prison into preparation for leadership.
- Everyday Survivors: Cancer patients, refugees, parents—those who turn hardship into new forms of life.

Toolbox: Practicing Resilience and Reinvention

1. Reflection Prompt: Recall a time you faced difficulty. What strength emerged in you that you didn't know you had?
2. Inquiry Exercise: What old belief or identity might you need to release to reinvent yourself?
3. Commitment Practice: Choose one current challenge. Write three possible ways it could become an opportunity for growth.

Integration with the 4 Layers of Transformation
- Conscious Layer: Build stress-regulating habits (sleep, exercise, mindfulness).
- Preconscious Layer: Replace limiting beliefs with empowering ones.
- Unconscious Layer: Work through grief and fear so they don't sabotage reinvention.
- Existential Layer: Choose to frame hardship as a chance to grow and create anew.

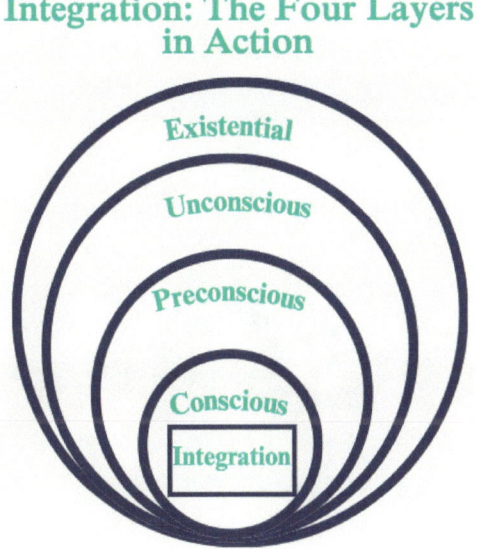

Closing Narrative

Miguel didn't play the piano the way he once had; rather, in his music now, people heard not just skill; but resilience, courage, and rebirth.

Resilience isn't about avoiding storms. It's about becoming someone new because of them.

And in reinvention, greatness is not just preserved—it is multiplied.

References

- Doidge, N. (2007). The Brain That Changes Itself. Viking.
- Dweck, C. S. (2006). Mindset: The New Psychology of Success. Random House.
- Meichenbaum, D. (2007). Stress Inoculation Training. In Lehrer, Woolfolk, & Sime (Eds.), Principles and Practice of Stress Management. Guilford Press.
- Park, C. L. (2010). Making sense of the meaning literature. Psychological Bulletin, 136(2), 257–301.
- Tedeschi, R. G., & Calhoun, L. G. (1996). The Posttraumatic Growth Inventory. Journal of Traumatic Stress, 9(3), 455–471.

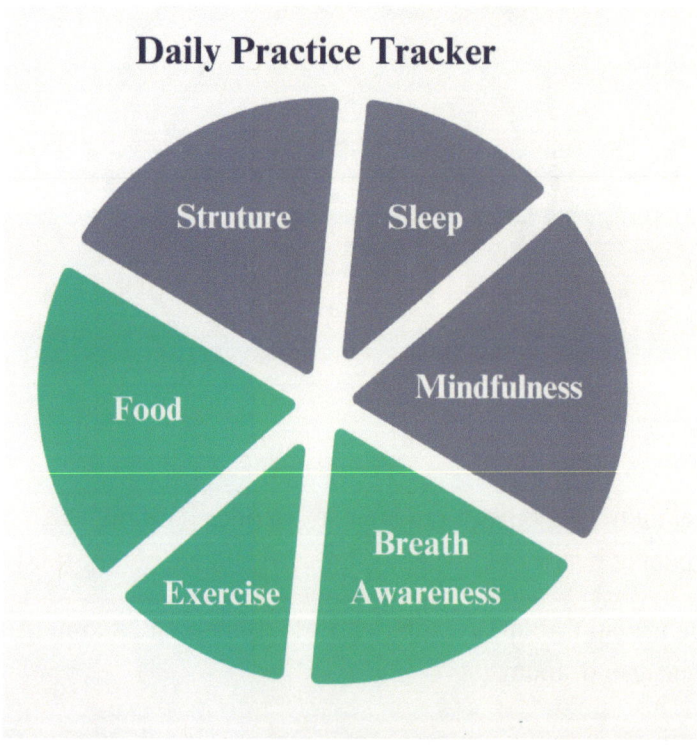

Part IV: Living as the Best

Chapter 11—The Purpose Beyond Self

The Story: The Teacher Who Stayed

In a small rural town, a young teacher was offered a high-paying job in the city. She considered leaving—better pay, more prestige. However, when she looked at her students, many of whom were the first in their families to read, she knew: *'If I go, who will stay?'*

Decades later, the town had leaders, doctors, and artists—all former students of hers. She never made headlines, but her purpose beyond self, echoed in generations.

Conversation: Mardoche and Karen

Karen: Purpose is the deepest motivator, but when it's only about the self, it can collapse into ego or emptiness.

Mardoche: Yes. The highest purpose is always beyond self. It's when our work contributes to something larger—community, humanity, even future generations.

Karen: And that doesn't always mean fame. Sometimes purpose beyond self is raising a child, planting a garden, or mentoring one person.

Mardoche: At the conscious level, it shows as service in daily actions. At the preconscious level, it's challenging schemas that equate worth with individual achievement. At the unconscious level, it's integrating drives of competition and fear. And at the existential layer, it's choosing contribution as the ultimate meaning.

Karen: That's why those with a purpose beyond self, radiate something different. They don't just succeed—they matter.

Circle of Relationships

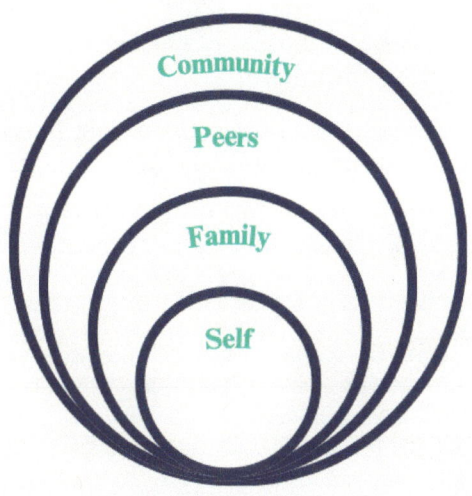

Science of Purpose Beyond Self

1. Eudaimonic Wellbeing – Purposeful living predicts health and longevity beyond hedonic pleasure (Ryff & Singer, 1998).
2. Transcendence and Flourishing – Maslow (1969) later revised his hierarchy, placing self-transcendence above self-actualization.
3. Contribution and Meaning – Giving and serving increase happiness more than receiving (Dunn, Aknin, & Norton, 2008).
4. Ikigai (Japanese Concept) – A life worth living lies at the intersection of love, skill, need, and reward.
5. Leadership and Legacy – Transformational leaders inspire through vision and service (Bass & Riggio, 2006).

Case Studies

- Viktor Frankl: Found meaning by serving fellow prisoners.
- Jane Goodall: Dedicated her life to protecting species and ecosystems.

- Everyday Givers: Parents, mentors, volunteers whose quiet service shapes futures.

Toolbox: Expanding Purpose
1. Reflection Prompt: What cause, person, or community would be poorer if you did not contribute?
2. Inquiry Exercise: If all your needs were met, what would you devote your energy to?
3. Commitment Practice: Identify one action this week that benefits someone beyond yourself.

Purpose Beyond Self: Ladder of Purpose

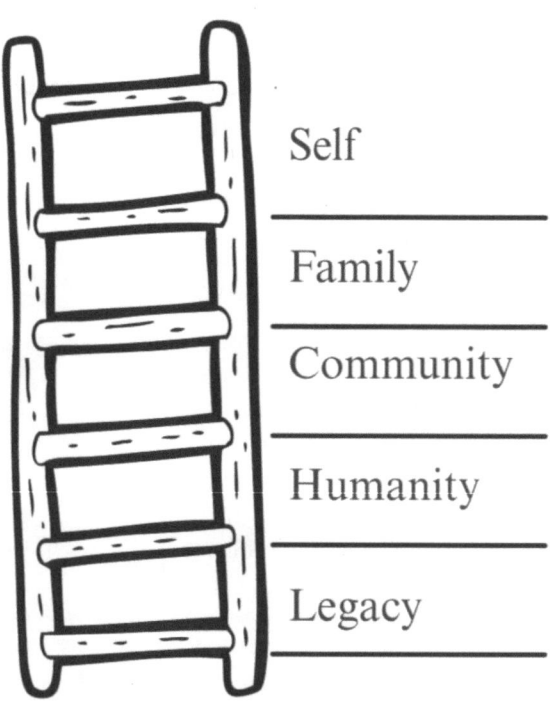

Integration with the 4 Layers of Transformation
- Conscious Layer: Practice acts of service daily.
- Preconscious Layer: Challenge the schema that worth = self-achievement.
- Unconscious Layer: Transform competition and fear into cooperation.
- Existential Layer: Choose contribution as the deepest meaning.

Closing Narrative

The teacher's salary was modest, her recognition quiet; yet her impact reverberated through the lives she touched.

The very best are not remembered only for what they achieved, but for what they gave.

And purpose beyond self is where excellence becomes legacy.

References
- Bass, B. M., & Riggio, R. E. (2006). Transformational Leadership. Lawrence Erlbaum.
- Dunn, E. W., Aknin, L. B., & Norton, M. I. (2008). Spending money on others promotes happiness. Science, 319(5870), 1687–1688.
- Maslow, A. H. (1969). The farther reaches of human nature. Journal of Transpersonal Psychology, 1(1), 1–9.
- Ryff, C. D., & Singer, B. (1998). The contours of positive human health. Psychological Inquiry, 9(1), 1–28.

Chapter 12—Integration: The Four Layers in Action

The Story: The Athlete Who Finally Won

Daniel had the discipline, he trained every day (conscious layer). He had worked with therapists to shift his limiting beliefs (preconscious layer). He had uncovered hidden fears of failure from his childhood (unconscious layer); yet he still fell short.

One day, reflecting with his coach, he asked: *'What does winning mean to me?'* In that moment, he realized victory wasn't about medals; rather, it was about embodying his deepest values of courage, perseverance, and service (existential layer).

From then on, Daniel competed differently. He didn't just win races. He became whole.

Conversation: Mardoche and Karen

Mardoche: Integration is the moment when the four layers stop being separate steps, and start becoming a way of life.

Karen: Exactly. Without integration, people can get stuck, endlessly working on habits, or lost in beliefs, or tangled in the unconscious.

Mardoche: But integration means weaving it all together. The conscious gives structure. The preconscious provides insight. The unconscious offers depth. And the existential ties it all to purpose.

Karen: That's when transformation is no longer a project, and becomes identity.

Science of Integration

1. Holistic Change – Behavior change lasts when it integrates habits, beliefs, unconscious processes, and meaning (Prochaska & DiClemente, 1983).
2. Narrative Identity – People who integrate life events into coherent meaning experience greater wellbeing (McAdams, 2001).
3. Psychodynamic Integration – Working through unconscious material leads to ego strength and resilience (Blatt & Levy, 2003).
4. Existential Psychology – Meaning-centered living sustains transformation beyond symptom relief (Yalom, 1980).
5. Systems Theory – Human growth requires integration across layers—physical, psychological, relational, existential (Bronfenbrenner, 1979).

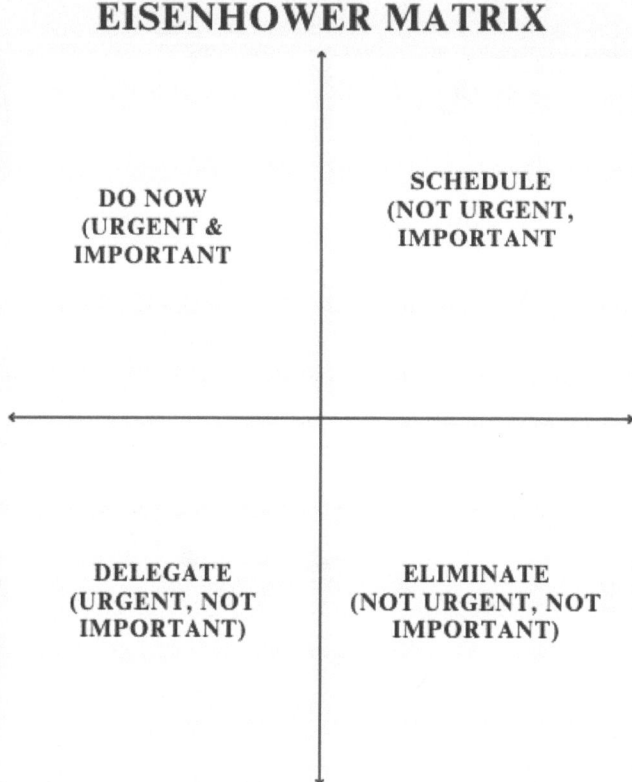

Case Studies

- Malcolm X: Transformed from street hustler to leader by integrating discipline, new beliefs, unconscious wounds, and existential purpose.
- Therapy Clients: Outcomes improve most when therapy combines conscious tools, preconscious reframing, unconscious work, and existential integration.
- Everyday Lives: Parents, leaders, healers who become consistent, insightful, self-aware, and purposeful all at once.

Toolbox: Practicing Integration

1. Reflection Prompt: Which of the four layers have you spent the most time on? Which have you avoided?
2. Inquiry Exercise: In your current challenge, how would you address it at all four layers?
3. Commitment Practice: Write an 'integration plan' that includes one practice at each layer.

Integration with the 4 Layers of Transformation (Meta-Reflection)

- Conscious Layer: Provides daily structure.
- Preconscious Layer: Offers insight into patterns.
- Unconscious Layer: Brings depth and hidden truths.
- Existential Layer: Connects everything to meaning and choice.

Together: Integration is not just adding them; rather, it's weaving them into a unified way of being.

Closing Narrative

Daniel didn't just run faster when he integrated the four layers. He ran freer, lighter, and truer.

Integration is the art of becoming whole; and wholeness is the hallmark of the very best.

References

- Blatt, S. J., & Levy, K. N. (2003). Attachment theory, psychoanalysis, personality development. Psychoanalytic Inquiry, 23(1), 102–150.
- Bronfenbrenner, U. (1979). The Ecology of Human Development. Harvard University Press.
- McAdams, D. P. (2001). The psychology of life stories. Review of General Psychology, 5(2), 100–122.
- Prochaska, J. O., & DiClemente, C. C. (1983). Stages and processes of self-change. Journal of Consulting and Clinical Psychology, 51(3), 390–395.
- Yalom, I. D. (1980). Existential Psychotherapy. Basic Books.

Part V: The Virtues of Greatness

Chapter 13—Legacy: Leaving What Lasts

The Story: The Builder's Gift

An architect was once asked why he spent years designing a bridge that would outlast him. He replied: 'Because one day, a child will cross this bridge, and they'll never know my name; but they'll arrive safely because of me.'

Years later, that bridge carried thousands daily. His name was forgotten, but his legacy remained in steel, stone, and lives touched.

Conversation: Mardoche and Karen

Karen: Legacy is what continues after us, but it's not just reputation; rather, it's impact.

Mardoche: Yes. Some think legacy is about being remembered. However, the truest legacy is living in ways that outlive memory.

Karen: Exactly. And legacy isn't only for the famous. Every parent, every teacher, every neighbor leaves a legacy in small acts of love and courage.

Mardoche: At the conscious layer, legacy is daily habits that ripple forward. At the preconscious layer, it's challenging beliefs like 'I don't matter.' At the unconscious level, it's freeing ourselves from fears of insignificance. And at the existential layer, it's choosing to live as though our actions echo into eternity.

Karen: Which they do. Whether we see it or not.

Science of Legacy

1. Generativity (Erikson, 1950) – Midlife development centers on caring for the next generation.
2. Transcendence of Mortality (Becker, 1973) – Legacy serves as a way to face mortality with courage and meaning.

3. Ripple Effect of Small Acts – Kindness spreads in networks up to three degrees (Fowler & Christakis, 2010).
4. Intergenerational Transmission – Values, resilience, and trauma are passed down across generations (Kellermann, 2001).
5. Purpose and Longevity – A strong sense of legacy predicts longer, healthier lives (Hill & Turiano, 2014).

Case Studies

- Viktor Frankl: His writings continue to save lives long after his.
- Maya Angelou: Her words inspire generations she never met.
- Everyday Citizens: Volunteers, caregivers, mentors whose ripple effects create lasting change.

Toolbox: Shaping Your Legacy

1. Reflection Prompt: If today were your last day, what would you want your legacy to be?
2. Inquiry Exercise: What values do you want to pass on—to children, students, or colleagues?
3. Commitment Practice: Write a 'Legacy Letter' to someone you love, sharing the lessons and values you hope they carry forward.

Integration with the 4 Layers of Transformation

- Conscious Layer: Daily choices create ripples.
- Preconscious Layer: Replace 'I don't matter' with 'Every act matters.'
- Unconscious Layer: Face mortality, insignificance, and integrate them with meaning.
- Existential Layer: Choose to live as if life's purpose is contribution, not consumption.

Closing Narrative

The bridge-builder never sought fame; yet his work carried generations forward.

Legacy is not about what we take with us; rather, it's about what we leave behind.

And when the four layers are integrated into a life of purpose, resilience, connection, and service, the legacy we leave is not just memory, but transformation.

References

- Becker, E. (1973). The Denial of Death. Free Press.
- Erikson, E. H. (1950). Childhood and Society. Norton.
- Fowler, J. H., & Christakis, N. A. (2010). Cooperative behavior cascades in human networks. PNAS, 107(12), 5334–5338.
- Hill, P. L., & Turiano, N. A. (2014). Purpose in life as a predictor of mortality. Psychological Science, 25(7), 1482–1486.
- Kellermann, N. P. (2001). Transmission of Holocaust trauma. Psychiatry, 64(3), 256–267.

Chapter 14—Courage: Facing Fear and Acting Anyway

The Story: The Firefighter's Choice

When the alarm rang, Captain Alvarez led his team into a burning building. Smoke clouded his vision, flames cracked the ceiling, and fear surged through his chest. Later he admitted: *'I was terrified. But my men were behind me, and a child was inside. Fear didn't disappear, it walked with me, but I walked anyway.'*

That is courage, and it is not the absence of fear, but action in its presence.

Conversation: Mardoche and Karen

Karen: People think courage means not being afraid. But the bravest people I've met are full of fear.

Mardoche: Exactly. The difference is they don't let fear decide. Courage is choosing values over comfort.

Karen: And it shows up everywhere: speaking truth when silence is safer, trying again after failure, and loving when rejection is possible.

Mardoche: At the conscious layer, courage is building habits of small risks. At the preconscious layer, it's rewriting schemas like 'fear means stop.' At the unconscious layer, it's facing the buried terrors that shape our defenses. And at the existential layer, it's choosing to live authentically, even in the face of death.

Karen: Which is why courage isn't just a virtue; rather, the doorway to all the others.

Science of Courage

1. Neurobiology of Fear – The amygdala triggers fear, but the prefrontal cortex regulates response (LeDoux, 1996).
2. Exposure and Habituation – Gradual exposure reduces fear response and builds courage (Foa & Kozak, 1986).
3. Moral Courage – Choosing to act on values despite risk predicts leadership and integrity (Sekerka & Bagozzi, 2007).
4. Post-Traumatic Growth – Courage in facing trauma can lead to growth and resilience (Tedeschi & Calhoun, 1996).
5. Small Acts of Courage – Everyday micro-courage strengthens confidence over time (Rate, Clarke, Lindsay, & Sternberg, 2007).

Case Studies

- Rosa Parks: One act of refusal reshaped history.
- Malala Yousafzai: Courage in education advocacy despite mortal risk.
- Everyday People: Survivors, parents, leaders who act despite fear.

Toolbox: Building Courage

1. Reflection Prompt: What fear is currently holding you back?
2. Inquiry Exercise: If you acted with courage, what would you do differently today?
3. Commitment Practice: Create a 'Courage Ladder'—list small fears from easiest to hardest. Start with the smallest, and climb.

Integration with the 4 Layers of Transformation

- Conscious Layer: Take daily small risks.
- Preconscious Layer: Challenge schemas that say fear = failure.
- Unconscious Layer: Explore hidden fears, repressed anxieties.
- Existential Layer: Choose values and meaning over comfort.

Together: Courage is the fuel that powers transformation across all four layers.

Closing Narrative

Captain Alvarez wasn't fearless. He was afraid; yet he still stepped forward.

The best don't wait for fear to vanish. They walk with it, act anyway, and in doing so, they build a life defined not by safety, but by strength.

References

- Foa, E. B., & Kozak, M. J. (1986). Emotional processing of fear: Exposure to corrective information. Psychological Bulletin, 99(1), 20–35.
- LeDoux, J. (1996). The Emotional Brain. Simon & Schuster.
- Rate, C. R., Clarke, J. A., Lindsay, D. R., & Sternberg, R. J. (2007). Implicit theories of courage. Journal of Positive Psychology, 2(2), 80–98.
- Sekerka, L. E., & Bagozzi, R. P. (2007). Moral courage in organizations. Business Ethics: A European Review, 16(2), 132–149.
- Tedeschi, R. G., & Calhoun, L. G. (1996). The Posttraumatic Growth Inventory. Journal of Traumatic Stress, 9(3), 455–471.

Chapter 15 —Creativity: Innovation as Path to Greatness

The Story: The Chef Who Reinvented Tradition

In Paris, Chef Amara inherited a family restaurant known for classic recipes; but instead of repeating tradition, she experimented: spices from Morocco, techniques from Japan, and plating like art. Critics at first dismissed her. However, soon, lines formed around the block.

Her genius wasn't in rejecting tradition, but in transforming it. Creativity made her unforgettable.

Conversation: Mardoche and Karen

Mardoche: Creativity is often mistaken as a gift. But it's really a discipline, a way of seeing differently.

Karen: Exactly. It's not limited to artists. A parent telling bedtime stories, a scientist testing new hypotheses, and a leader finding new solutions—all are acts of creativity.

Mardoche: At the conscious layer, creativity is cultivated through daily practice and habits. At the preconscious layer, it's freeing ourselves from rigid schemas. At the unconscious layer, it's tapping into dreamlike associations and intuition. And at the existential layer, creativity is self-expression and meaning-making.

Karen: The very best don't just repeat; rather, they create, and creation is how they leave their mark.

Science of Creativity

1. Divergent Thinking – Creativity involves generating multiple solutions, not just one (Guilford, 1967).
2. Flow States – Deep immersion leads to breakthroughs (Csikszentmihalyi, 1990).

3. Neuroscience of Creativity – The interplay of the default mode network and executive control network drives innovation (Beaty et al., 2016).
4. Incubation Effect – Stepping away from problems enhances creative solutions (Sio & Ormerod, 2009).
5. Resilience and Creativity – Adversity can fuel creative adaptation (Forgeard, 2013).

Case Studies

- Steve Jobs: Integrated technology and design into transformative products.
- Maya Angelou: Wove poetry, autobiography, and activism into a new form of art.
- Everyday Innovators: Teachers, parents, community leaders who craft solutions to survive and thrive.

Toolbox: Cultivating Creativity

1. Reflection Prompt: What's one area of your life where you're stuck in routine? How might you reimagine it?
2. Inquiry Exercise: Ask: 'What if I did the opposite?' or 'What if there were no rules?'
3. Commitment Practice: Dedicate 15 minutes daily to free creation—writing, sketching, problem-solving. No judgment, only output.

Integration with the 4 Layers of Transformation

- Conscious Layer: Practice creativity through daily habits and time blocks.
- Preconscious Layer: Challenge rigid schemas and 'shoulds.'
- Unconscious Layer: Use dreams, intuition, and free association to unlock hidden ideas.
- Existential Layer: Express your deepest values and vision through creation.

Together: Creativity makes life not just efficient, but extraordinary.

Closing Narrative

Chef Amara's diners didn't just eat. They experienced wonder.

Creativity transforms the ordinary into the extraordinary; and those who dare to create don't just live in the world; rather, they remake it.

References

- Beaty, R. E., Benedek, M., Kaufman, S. B., & Silvia, P. J. (2016). Default and executive network coupling supports creative idea production. Scientific Reports, 5, 10964.
- Csikszentmihalyi, M. (1990). Flow: The Psychology of Optimal Experience. Harper & Row.
- Forgeard, M. J. C. (2013). Perceiving benefits after adversity: The relationship between self-reported posttraumatic growth and creativity. Psychology of Aesthetics, Creativity, and the Arts, 7(3), 245–264.
- Guilford, J. P. (1967). The Nature of Human Intelligence. McGraw-Hill.
- Sio, U. N., & Ormerod, T. C. (2009). Does incubation enhance problem solving? Psychological Bulletin, 135(1), 94–120.

Chapter 16—Humility: The Ground of True Excellence

The Story: The Scientist Who Shared the Prize

When Dr. Lee received a prestigious award for her groundbreaking research, she surprised everyone. Instead of speaking about her genius, she listed every mentor, lab partner, and assistant who made the work possible. Reporters said her humility overshadowed the prize itself.

Her legacy was not only discovery, but also dignity.

Conversation: Mardoche and Karen

Karen: Many equate greatness with ego, but the most impactful people I've known are deeply humble.

Mardoche: Right. Humility doesn't mean self-erasure. It means seeing oneself accurately, through one's strengths, limitations, and interdependence.

Karen: And humility allows learning. A proud mind closes; while 9a humble mind expands.

Mardoche: At the conscious layer, humility shows up in listening and daily practices of gratitude. At the preconscious layer, it means challenging schemas like 'I must always be right.' At the unconscious level, it's examining defenses that protect fragile self-esteem. At the existential layer, humility is choosing service over self-importance.

Karen: Which makes humility not weakness, but strength.

Science of Humility

1. Leadership Research – Humble leaders inspire trust, collaboration, and higher performance (Collins, 2001).

2. Psychological Growth – Humility is linked to openness to feedback and personal growth (Tangney, 2000).
3. Social Connection – Humble people form stronger relationships and greater empathy (Rowatt et al., 2006).
4. Intellectual Humility – Willingness to revise beliefs predicts better reasoning and reduced polarization (Krumrei-Mancuso & Rouse, 2016).
5. Spiritual Traditions – Nearly every wisdom tradition views humility as a foundation of character.

Case Studies

- Abraham Lincoln: Known for humility and willingness to admit mistakes.
- Mother Teresa: Her greatness lay in service, not recognition.
- Everyday Examples: Teachers, nurses, and community leaders who lift others quietly.

Toolbox: Practicing Humility

1. Reflection Prompt: When was the last time you were wrong? What did you learn?
2. Inquiry Exercise: Whose help have you minimized or ignored? How can you honor it?
3. Commitment Practice: Each day, practice one act of gratitude or acknowledgment of others.

Integration with the 4 Layers of Transformation

- Conscious Layer: Practice gratitude, listening, acknowledgment.
- Preconscious Layer: Challenge schemas of superiority or perfectionism.
- Unconscious Layer: Work through defenses that mask insecurity.

- Existential Layer: Embrace humility as the soil for meaning, connection, and growth.

Together: Humility grounds greatness, ensuring it serves, not inflates.

Closing Narrative

Dr. Lee's award speech was not about her, but about others.

Humility is the paradox of the very best: those who are truly great rarely think of themselves as great.

References

- Collins, J. (2001). Good to Great. HarperBusiness.
- Krumrei-Mancuso, E. J., & Rouse, S. V. (2016). Intellectual humility. Personality and Individual Differences, 97, 165–172.
- Rowatt, W. C., et al. (2006). Associations between humility, personality, and prosocial behavior. Journal of Positive Psychology, 1(4), 227–235.
- Tangney, J. P. (2000). Humility: Theoretical perspectives. Journal of Social and Clinical Psychology, 19(1), 70–82.

Chapter 17—Service: Turning Greatness Into Contribution

The Story: The Doctor Who Stayed Late

Dr. Patel finished his shift at the hospital. Exhausted, he was about to leave when a nurse whispered: *'One more patient is waiting, scared and alone.'*

He stayed, he listened, and he held the patient's hand.

The patient later said: 'That moment of kindness meant more than the medicine.'

Greatness isn't always about achievement, yet always about service.

Conversation: Mardoche and Karen

Karen: Service is the bridge between personal excellence and collective impact.

Mardoche: Yes. Without service, greatness risks becoming self-centered. But service transforms achievement into contribution.

Karen: At the conscious layer, service looks like daily acts of kindness. At the preconscious layer, it challenges the schema that success is only about 'me.' At the unconscious layer, it heals the wounds of isolation by reconnecting us; while at the existential layer, service becomes meaning itself.

Mardoche: Which is why the most fulfilled lives are not about accumulation, but about giving.

Science of Service

1. Altruism and Wellbeing – Acts of service increase happiness, reduce stress, and improve health (Post, 2005).

2. Helper's High – Service activates brain reward centers, producing joy and resilience (Moll et al., 2006).
3. Social Capital – Communities with higher rates of service and volunteering show greater trust and wellbeing (Putnam, 2000).
4. Meaning and Mortality – Serving others provides existential meaning, buffering fear of death (Wong, 2010).
5. Ripple Effect – Service inspires observers to serve, creating exponential impact (Fowler & Christakis, 2010).

Case Studies

- Albert Schweitzer: Physician who dedicated his life to medical missions in Africa.
- Oseola McCarty: A washerwoman who donated her life savings to fund scholarships.
- Everyday Service: Neighbors helping neighbors, mentors guiding youth, parents serving children.

Toolbox: Practicing Service

1. Reflection Prompt: Who in your life needs your help right now?
2. Inquiry Exercise: What skills, resources, or time can you share with others?
3. Commitment Practice: Choose one act of service this week—small or large—and do it without expecting recognition.

Integration with the 4 Layers of Transformation

- Conscious Layer: Practice service through daily actions.
- Preconscious Layer: Challenge beliefs that service = weakness.
- Unconscious Layer: Heal loneliness by connecting through giving.
- Existential Layer: Make service a cornerstone of your purpose.

Together: Service transforms self-growth into collective flourishing.

Closing Narrative

Dr. Patel's greatness was not measured in awards, but in presence.

The best don't just shine for themselves; rather, they light the way for others.

References

- Fowler, J. H., & Christakis, N. A. (2010). Cooperative behavior cascades in human networks. PNAS, 107(12), 5334–5338.
- Moll, J., et al. (2006). Human fronto–mesolimbic networks guide decisions about charitable donation. PNAS, 103(42), 15623–15628.
- Post, S. G. (2005). Altruism, happiness, and health: It's good to be good. International Journal of Behavioral Medicine, 12(2), 66–77.
- Putnam, R. D. (2000). Bowling Alone: The Collapse and Revival of American Community. Simon & Schuster.
- Wong, P. T. P. (2010). Meaning therapy: An integrative and positive existential psychotherapy. Journal of Contemporary Psychotherapy, 40(2), 85–93.

Chapter 18—Presence: Mastering the Now

The Story: The Pianist on Stage

During her recital, Hana began to panic. Her thoughts raced: *'What if I make a mistake?'* But then she looked at the piano keys, took a breath, and sank into the music.

She stopped performing for the audience, and started playing for the moment; and the hall then filled with silence, and then with thunderous applause.

Her presence turned performance into transcendence.

Conversation: Mardoche and Karen

Karen: Presence is the art of showing up fully, without being hijacked by the past or dragged by the future.

Mardoche: Right. Many confuse presence with relaxation. However, presence can also be intense, and it's about being awake.

Karen: At the conscious layer, presence means practices like meditation, mindfulness, and focus. At the preconscious layer, it requires noticing the schemas that pull us into 'what ifs.' At the unconscious layer, presence emerges when repressed material is acknowledged instead of avoided. At the existential layer, presence is the realization that this moment is life itself.

Mardoche: The very best don't just work hard; rather, they are fully here, now.

Science of Presence

1. Mindfulness Research – Presence improves attention, reduces stress, and enhances wellbeing (Kabat-Zinn, 1990).
2. Flow Theory – Being absorbed in the present leads to optimal performance (Csikszentmihalyi, 1990).

3. Attentional Control – Presence strengthens the prefrontal cortex's regulation of distraction (Posner & Rothbart, 2007).
4. Trauma and Presence – Mindfulness helps trauma survivors anchor in the present safely (van der Kolk, 2014).
5. Relationships and Presence – Deep presence fosters intimacy, trust, and empathy (Brown, 2012).

Case Studies

- Eckhart Tolle: His teachings on The Power of Now influenced millions.
- Athletes: Peak performance consistently linked to presence in competition.
- Everyday People: Parents who truly listen, friends who give undivided attention.

Toolbox: Practicing Presence

1. Reflection Prompt: When was the last time you were fully in the moment?
2. Inquiry Exercise: What distracts you most often—past regrets, future worries, or present noise?
3. Commitment Practice: Practice 'micro-presence': 60 seconds of full attention to breath, sound, or sensation, several times a day.

Integration with the 4 Layers of Transformation

- Conscious Layer: Use mindfulness, breathing, focus practices.
- Preconscious Layer: Challenge schemas of worry and perfectionism.
- Unconscious Layer: Recognize and release old patterns that hijack attention.
- Existential Layer: Live as though the present moment is precious.

Together: Presence transforms time into life, and life into transformation.

Closing Narrative

Hana's music was not just heard; rather, it was felt, because she was fully there.

The very best don't chase the future; rather, they master the now.

References

- Brown, B. (2012). Daring Greatly. Gotham.
- Csikszentmihalyi, M. (1990). Flow: The Psychology of Optimal Experience. Harper & Row.
- Kabat-Zinn, J. (1990). Full Catastrophe Living. Dell.
- Posner, M. I., & Rothbart, M. K. (2007). Research on attention networks. Annual Review of Psychology, 58, 1–23.
- van der Kolk, B. (2014). The Body Keeps the Score. Viking.

Transcendence

Work & Service

Relationships

Self

MEANING PYRAMID

Chapter 19—Love: The Greatest Force in Human Growth

The Story: The Teacher's Gift

In a crowded classroom, Mr. Morales noticed a shy student who rarely spoke. Instead of pushing him, he offered patience, encouragement, and care.

Years later, that student returned, saying: 'You believed in me when no one else did; and that changed my life.'

It wasn't a grand act, but an act of love, and it transformed a life.

Conversation: Mardoche and Karen

Karen: Love is often reduced to romance, but in truth it's the energy that fuels human flourishing.

Mardoche: Yes. Love is seeing the worth in another, and acting to nurture it.

Karen: At the conscious layer, love is expressed through actions: listening, kindness, respect. At the preconscious layer, it requires challenging schemas like 'I am unworthy of love.' At the unconscious layer, it heals attachment wounds and defenses against intimacy. And at the existential layer, love becomes the very meaning of existence.

Mardoche: Which is why the very best are not just achievers; rather, they are lovers, in the deepest sense.

Science of Love

1. Attachment Theory – Secure love fosters resilience and exploration (Bowlby, 1988).
2. Neurobiology of Love – Oxytocin and dopamine systems drive bonding and trust (Carter, 1998).

3. Compassion Research – Loving-kindness meditation increases empathy, wellbeing, and prosocial behavior (Fredrickson et al., 2008).
4. Health Outcomes – Strong loving relationships predict longer life and lower illness rates (Holt-Lunstad et al., 2010).
5. Universal Love – Altruistic love fosters intergroup cooperation and peace (Ricard, 2015).

Case Studies

- Nelson Mandela: Chose reconciliation over revenge, grounded in love
- Mother Teresa: Built her mission on radical love for the poor.
- Everyday Love: Parents, teachers, partners, and friends whose love builds resilience in others.

Toolbox: Practicing Love

1. Reflection Prompt: How do you show love to yourself? To others?
2. Inquiry Exercise: What core belief about love may be limiting your ability to give or receive it?
3. Commitment Practice: Practice one daily act of love—small or large—without expectation of return.

Integration with the 4 Layers of Transformation

- Conscious Layer: Practice daily loving actions.
- Preconscious Layer: Challenge schemas of unworthiness or mistrust.
- Unconscious Layer: Heal repressed wounds of abandonment or betrayal.
- Existential Layer: Live as though love is the ultimate purpose.

Together: Love integrates all layers of transformation into connection and meaning.

Closing Narrative

Mr. Morales didn't give wealth or fame—he gave love.

The very best change the world not by power, but by love.

References

- Bowlby, J. (1988). A Secure Base: Parent-Child Attachment and Healthy Human Development. Basic Books.
- Carter, C. S. (1998). Neuroendocrine perspectives on social attachment. Psychoneuroendocrinology, 23(8), 779–818.
- Fredrickson, B. L., et al. (2008). Open hearts build lives: Positive emotions induced through loving-kindness meditation. Journal of Personality and Social Psychology, 95(5), 1045–1062.
- Holt-Lunstad, J., et al. (2010). Social relationships and mortality risk: A meta-analytic review. PLoS Medicine, 7(7), e1000316.
- Ricard, M. (2015). Altruism: The Power of Compassion to Change Yourself and the World. Little, Brown.

Chapter 20—Wisdom: Integrating Knowledge Into Life

The Story: The Elder's Answer

In a village council, the people argued fiercely about a new law. Finally, the elder spoke: *'Knowledge tells us what we can do; while Wisdom tells us whether to do it, when, and how.'*

The crowd grew silent, decisions changed, and the village thrived.

Wisdom is not knowing more; rather, it's living better.

Conversation: Mardoche and Karen

Karen: Knowledge is everywhere now, but wisdom is rare.

Mardoche: Yes. Wisdom is the integration of knowledge, experience, and compassion.

Karen: At the conscious layer, wisdom is applying knowledge to daily choices. At the preconscious layer, it's revising schemas shaped by pride or shortsightedness. At the unconscious layer, it's recognizing hidden biases and defenses. And at the existential layer, wisdom is living with purpose, guided by meaning.

Mardoche: That's why the wisest don't just inform; rather, they transform.

Science of Wisdom

1. Developmental Psychology – Wisdom develops through life reflection and integration (Erikson, 1982).
2. Cognitive Studies – Wise reasoning includes perspective-taking, humility, and balancing interests (Grossmann, 2017).
3. Neuroscience – Prefrontal cortex and default mode network support reflective judgment (Meeks & Jeste, 2009).

4. Cultural Universality – Every culture honors wisdom as essential to leadership (Ardelt, 2003).
5. Wisdom and Wellbeing – Greater wisdom correlates with resilience and life satisfaction (Jeste et al., 2010).

Case Studies

- King Solomon: Famous for discerning wisdom.
- Mahatma Gandhi: Integrated truth, nonviolence, and justice into action.
- Everyday Elders: Grandparents, mentors, spiritual leaders shaping lives with perspective.

Toolbox: Practicing Wisdom

1. Reflection Prompt: What knowledge do I have that I am not yet applying wisely?
2. Inquiry Exercise: Ask: 'What would a wise elder do in this situation?'
3. Commitment Practice: Begin a 'Wisdom Journal'—write one life lesson learned each week.

Integration with the 4 Layers of Transformation

- Conscious Layer: Apply knowledge to choices.
- Preconscious Layer: Challenge schemas of arrogance or shortsightedness.
- Unconscious Layer: Uncover biases and hidden drivers.
- Existential Layer: Live guided by purpose, beyond self.

Together: Wisdom is the compass for lasting greatness.

Closing Narrative

The elder didn't win by facts, but by wisdom.

The very best don't just accumulate knowledge; rather, they embody wisdom.

References

- Ardelt, M. (2003). Empirical assessment of a three-dimensional wisdom scale. Research on Aging, 25(3), 275–324.
- Erikson, E. H. (1982). The Life Cycle Completed. Norton.
- Grossmann, I. (2017). Wisdom in context. Perspectives on Psychological Science, 12(2), 233–257.
- Jeste, D. V., et al. (2010). Wisdom: A neuroscience perspective. Archives of General Psychiatry, 67(4), 355–365.
- Meeks, T. W., & Jeste, D. V. (2009). Neurobiology of wisdom. Archives of General Psychiatry, 66(4), 355–365.

Chapter 21—Resilience: Rising Strong from Setbacks

The Story: The Runner Who Fell

In the middle of a marathon, Javier tripped and fell hard. Bloodied, he wanted to quit. However, he stood up, limped, then found his stride again. He finished last but received the loudest applause.

Resilience isn't about never falling; rather, it's about always rising.

Conversation: Mardoche and Karen

Karen: Many people think resilience means toughness, but it's really flexibility.

Mardoche: Exactly. It's not about resisting stress—it's about adapting, recovering, and growing.

Karen: At the conscious layer, resilience is built through routines, sleep, exercise, and healthy coping. At the preconscious layer, it means challenging schemas like 'failure is permanent.' At the unconscious layer, resilience requires working through defenses against pain. And at the existential layer, it means choosing meaning in suffering.

Mardoche: Which is why the very best are not the ones who never fail; rather, the ones who never stop.

Science of Resilience

1. Post-Traumatic Growth – Many individuals report greater strength and meaning after adversity (Tedeschi & Calhoun, 2004).
2. Protective Factors – Optimism, social support, and coping strategies buffer stress (Masten, 2001).

3. Neuroplasticity – Brains adapt and rewire after trauma, fostering recovery (Davidson & McEwen, 2012).
4. Resilience Training – Practices like mindfulness and CBT improve resilience (Southwick & Charney, 2018).
5. Community Resilience – Societies can recover stronger after crises when solidarity is high (Norris et al., 2008).

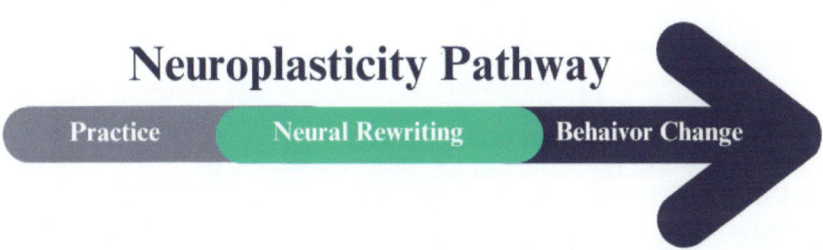

Case Studies

- Nelson Mandela: Imprisoned for 27 years, emerged as a unifier.
- Oprah Winfrey: Transformed childhood trauma into leadership and influence.
- Everyday Heroes: Survivors who rebuild lives after loss, illness, or disaster.

Toolbox: Building Resilience

1. Reflection Prompt: What was a past setback that made you stronger?
2. Inquiry Exercise: When you fall, what story do you tell yourself: 'I'm finished' or 'I'm learning'?
3. Commitment Practice: Practice one micro-resilience habit daily (deep breathing, gratitude, reaching out for support).

Integration with the 4 Layers of Transformation
- Conscious Layer: Build routines, habits, and healthy coping
- Preconscious Layer: Revise schemas that equate failure with weakness.
- Unconscious Layer: Process defenses and pain, rather than avoiding them.
- Existential Layer: Choose meaning in setbacks.

Together: Resilience turns wounds into wisdom, and pain into power.

Closing Narrative
Javier didn't win the race, but he won hearts.

The very best don't avoid hardship; rather, they rise stronger because of it.

References
- Davidson, R. J., & McEwen, B. S. (2012). Social influences on neuroplasticity. Nature Neuroscience, 15(5), 689–695.
- Masten, A. S. (2001). Ordinary magic: Resilience processes in development. American Psychologist, 56(3), 227–238.
- Norris, F. H., et al. (2008). Community resilience as a metaphor, theory, and set of capacities. American Journal of Community Psychology, 41(1-2), 127–150.
- Southwick, S. M., & Charney, D. S. (2018). Resilience: The Science of Mastering Life's Greatest Challenges. Cambridge University Press.
- Tedeschi, R. G., & Calhoun, L. G. (2004). Posttraumatic growth: Conceptual foundations and empirical evidence. Psychological Inquiry, 15(1), 1–18.

Chapter 22—Integrity: Living in Alignment with Truth

The Story: The Whistleblower's Choice

When Sarah discovered corruption in her company, she faced a choice: stay silent to protect her career, or speak the truth. She chose integrity. She lost her job, but gained her soul.

Years later, people remembered her not for her position, but for her courage to live in truth.

Conversation: Mardoche and Karen

Karen: Integrity is doing the right thing when no one is watching.

Mardoche: And it's more than honesty for it's also consistency between values, words, and actions.

Karen: At the conscious layer, integrity shows up in daily actions: keeping promises, speaking truth. At the preconscious layer, it means challenging schemas like 'success requires compromise of values.' At the unconscious layer, it's about examining hidden motives and defenses. At the existential layer, integrity is choosing to live authentically, aligned with ultimate purpose.

Mardoche: Which is why the very best are trusted, not because they're perfect, but because they're whole.

Science of Integrity

1. Moral Psychology – Integrity predicts trust and social cohesion (Aquino & Reed, 2002).
2. Wellbeing – Living aligned with values reduces stress and increases life satisfaction (Sheldon & Kasser, 2001).
3. Leadership – Integrity is the strongest predictor of long-term leadership effectiveness (Palanski & Yammarino, 2009).

4. Authenticity – Integrity overlaps with authenticity, linked to resilience and wellbeing (Kernis & Goldman, 2006).
5. Organizational Health – Cultures of integrity foster innovation and sustainability (Simons, 2002).

Case Studies

- Mahatma Gandhi: Lived 'truth-force' (satyagraha), aligning words and actions.
- Nelson Mandela: Maintained integrity even in prison, refusing bitterness.
- Everyday Integrity: Workers, parents, and leaders who choose truth over convenience.

Toolbox: Practicing Integrity

1. Reflection Prompt: Where am I out of alignment with my values?
2. Inquiry Exercise: What hidden belief tempts me to compromise truth?
3. Commitment Practice: Choose one value and live it consistently this week.

Integration with the 4 Layers of Transformation

- Conscious Layer: Keep promises, align actions with values.
- Preconscious Layer: Challenge schemas of compromise.
- Unconscious Layer: Examine hidden motives and defenses.
- Existential Layer: Live authentically, as a whole self.

Together: Integrity unites all layers into wholeness.

Closing Narrative

Sarah lost her career but gained something greater: She gained herself.

The very best don't just succeed; rather, they live in truth.

References

- Aquino, K., & Reed, A. (2002). The self-importance of moral identity. Journal of Personality and Social Psychology, 83(6), 1423–1440.
- Kernis, M. H., & Goldman, B. M. (2006). A multicomponent conceptualization of authenticity. Advances in Experimental Social Psychology, 38, 283–357.
- Palanski, M. E., & Yammarino, F. J. (2009). Integrity and leadership. Journal of Leadership & Organizational Studies, 16(1), 89–99.
- Sheldon, K. M., & Kasser, T. (2001). Goals, congruence, and well-being. Journal of Personality and Social Psychology, 80(1), 152–165.
- Simons, T. (2002). Behavioral integrity: The perceived alignment between managers' words and deeds. Human Relations, 55(3), 323–338.

Chapter 23—Curiosity: The Engine of Growth

The Story: The Child Who Asked Why

At age 6, Maya asked her teacher why the sky was blue. The teacher gave a simple answer. Maya asked again: *'But why?'* She kept asking, year after year, until she became an astrophysicist discovering new galaxies.

Curiosity didn't just give her answers; rather, it gave her a life.

Conversation: Mardoche and Karen

Karen: Curiosity is the spark of all learning and growth.

Mardoche: Yes. The best are not the ones who know most, but the ones who never stop asking.

Karen: At the conscious layer, curiosity is about seeking new knowledge and experiences. At the preconscious layer, it challenges limiting schemas like 'I shouldn't question things.' At the unconscious layer, curiosity helps us explore repressed material with openness. And at the existential layer, curiosity is a stance toward life itself: embracing mystery.

Mardoche: Which is why the very best are lifelong learners.

Science of Curiosity

1. Intrinsic Motivation – Curiosity drives deeper learning and persistence (Deci & Ryan, 1985).
2. Brain Reward Systems – Curiosity activates the dopaminergic system, enhancing memory (Gruber et al., 2014).
3. Exploration and Creativity – Curiosity predicts creativity and innovation (Kashdan & Silvia, 2009).
4. Resilience through Curiosity – Curious people handle uncertainty better (Kashdan et al., 2004).

5. Wellbeing – Curiosity enhances relationships and life satisfaction (Kashdan & Steger, 2007).

Case Studies

- Leonardo da Vinci: Endless curiosity fueled art, science, and invention.
- Marie Curie: Curiosity led to groundbreaking discoveries in radioactivity.
- Everyday Curiosity: Children exploring, adults learning new skills, elders staying mentally active.

Toolbox: Practicing Curiosity

1. Reflection Prompt: What do I most want to understand right now?
2. Inquiry Exercise: Ask 'Why?' five times about any challenge you face.
3. Commitment Practice: Each day, explore something new—an article, a skill, a conversation.

Integration with the 4 Layers of Transformation

- Conscious Layer: Seek new knowledge, experiment.
- Preconscious Layer: Challenge schemas against questioning.
- Unconscious Layer: Explore repressed material with openness.
- Existential Layer: Live with wonder at life's mysteries.

Together: Curiosity fuels the lifelong journey of becoming.

Closing Narrative

Maya's questions led her to galaxies.

The very best don't stop at answers; rather, they keep asking.

References

- Deci, E. L., & Ryan, R. M. (1985). Intrinsic Motivation and Self-Determination in Human Behavior. Springer.
- Gruber, M. J., et al. (2014). States of curiosity modulate hippocampus-dependent learning. Neuron, 84(2), 486–496.
- Kashdan, T. B., & Silvia, P. J. (2009). Curiosity and interest: The benefits of thriving on novelty. Positive Psychology, 4(5), 367–370.
- Kashdan, T. B., Rose, P., & Fincham, F. D. (2004). Curiosity and exploration: Facilitating positive subjective experiences and personal growth. Journal of Personality Assessment, 82(3), 291–305.
- Kashdan, T. B., & Steger, M. F. (2007). Curiosity and pathways to well-being. Journal of Research in Personality, 41(4), 987–1016.

Chapter 24—Discipline: The Structure of Freedom

The Story: The Violinist's Routine

Every morning at 5 a.m., Sofia practiced her violin scales. Rain or shine, tired or not, she played. Years later, when she stood on the stage of Carnegie Hall, the audience marveled at her brilliance.

Her freedom to improvise came from years of disciplined practice.

Conversation: Mardoche and Karen

Karen: People think discipline is restriction, but it's actually liberation.

Mardoche: Exactly. Discipline creates the structure that allows greatness to flourish.

Karen: At the conscious layer, discipline means building routines, habits, and accountability. At the preconscious layer, it's challenging schemas like 'I'll never follow through.' At the unconscious layer, it means working through resistance, procrastination, and self-sabotage. At the existential layer, discipline becomes devotion: aligning effort with purpose.

Mardoche: Which is why the very best don't wait for motivation; rather, they build discipline.

Science of Discipline

1. Self-Regulation Research – Discipline predicts success more strongly than IQ (Duckworth & Seligman, 2005).
2. Habit Formation – Daily repetition rewires the brain for automaticity (Lally et al., 2010).
3. Delayed Gratification – The famous 'marshmallow test' showed long-term benefits of discipline (Mischel, 2014).

4. Neurobiology – Prefrontal cortex governs self-control, strengthened by practice (Moffitt et al., 2011).
5. Wellbeing – Disciplined individuals report greater health, satisfaction, and resilience (Baumeister & Tierney, 2011).

Case Studies

- Serena Williams: Legendary work ethic built her tennis mastery.
- Benjamin Franklin: Designed a disciplined daily schedule for self-improvement.
- Everyday Discipline: Students, parents, and workers who show up consistently, day after day.

Toolbox: Practicing Discipline

1. Reflection Prompt: What area of my life most needs structure right now?
2. Inquiry Exercise: What belief or story makes me resist discipline?
3. Commitment Practice: Choose one keystone habit (exercise, journaling, reading) and commit for 30 days.

Integration with the 4 Layers of Transformation

- Conscious Layer: Build habits, routines, and accountability.
- Preconscious Layer: Challenge schemas of inconsistency or defeat.
- Unconscious Layer: Work through resistance and self-sabotage.
- Existential Layer: Align discipline with deeper meaning and purpose.

Together: Discipline turns intention into transformation.

Closing Narrative

Sofia's music was free because her life was disciplined.

The very best are not ruled by impulse; rather, they are guided by discipline.

References

- Baumeister, R. F., & Tierney, J. (2011). Willpower: Rediscovering the Greatest Human Strength. Penguin.
- Duckworth, A. L., & Seligman, M. E. (2005). Self-discipline outdoes IQ in predicting academic performance. Psychological Science, 16(12), 939–944.
- Lally, P., et al. (2010). How are habits formed: Modelling habit formation in the real world. European Journal of Social Psychology, 40(6), 998–1009.
- Mischel, W. (2014). The Marshmallow Test. Little, Brown.
- Moffitt, T. E., et al. (2011). A gradient of childhood self-control predicts health, wealth, and public safety. PNAS, 108(7), 2693–2698.

Chapter 25—Gratitude: The Science of Fulfillment

The Story: The Soldier's Letter

During the war, Daniel wrote home: 'I don't know what tomorrow holds, but today I'm grateful, for the sunrise, for my friends, and for being alive.'

Years later, after surviving, he said it was gratitude that gave him strength in the darkest days.

Gratitude doesn't erase suffering; rather, it transforms it.

Conversation: Mardoche and Karen

Karen: Gratitude is one of the most researched pathways to happiness.

Mardoche: Yes. And it's not just a feeling; rather, it's a practice, a lens through which we see life.

Karen: At the conscious layer, gratitude is expressed through journaling, thank-you notes, or reflection. At the preconscious layer, it challenges schemas like 'I never have enough.' At the unconscious layer, gratitude transforms hidden envy and resentment. At the existential layer, it becomes a worldview: life itself is a gift.

Mardoche: Which is why the very best don't just strive, they also give thanks.

Science of Gratitude

1. Positive Psychology – Gratitude journaling increases happiness and reduces depression (Emmons & McCullough, 2003).
2. Neurobiology – Gratitude activates brain regions linked to reward and bonding (Fox et al., 2015).
3. Physical Health – Gratitude practices improve sleep, immunity, and heart health (Mills et al., 2015).
4. Relationships – Expressing gratitude strengthens bonds and trust (Algoe et al., 2008).
5. Resilience – Gratitude buffers stress and fosters post-traumatic growth (Wood et al., 2010).

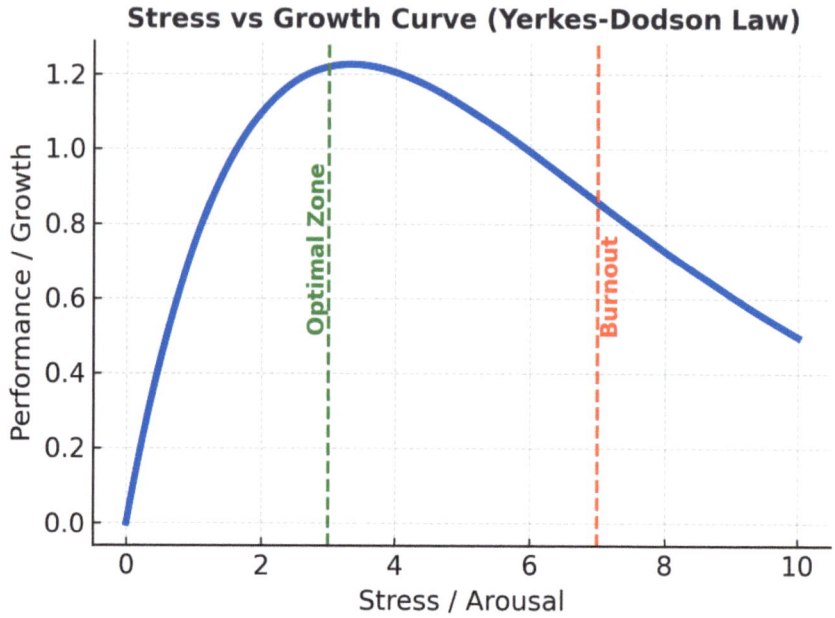

Case Studies

- Oprah Winfrey: Advocates gratitude journaling as a cornerstone of success.
- Holocaust Survivors: Many found meaning and strength in gratitude despite horror.
- Everyday Gratitude: Parents, workers, and friends who pause to say 'thank you.'

Toolbox: Practicing Gratitude

1. Reflection Prompt: What three things am I grateful for today?
2. Inquiry Exercise: What unconscious belief blinds me to life's gifts?
3. Commitment Practice: Start a gratitude journal—one entry daily for 30 days.

Integration with the 4 Layers of Transformation

- Conscious Layer: Write, speak, and act gratitude.
- Preconscious Layer: Challenge scarcity and entitlement schemas.
- Unconscious Layer: Heal envy, resentment, or unacknowledged blessings.
- Existential Layer: Live in gratitude for existence itself.

Together: Gratitude shifts life from striving to fulfillment.

Closing Narrative

Daniel survived because he gave thanks for life itself.

The very best don't just achieve, they are also grateful.

References

- Algoe, S. B., et al. (2008). Beyond reciprocity: Gratitude and relationships. Emotion, 8(3), 425–429.
- Emmons, R. A., & McCullough, M. E. (2003). Counting blessings versus burdens: An experimental investigation. Journal of Personality and Social Psychology, 84(2), 377–389.
- Fox, G. R., et al. (2015). Neural correlates of gratitude. Frontiers in Psychology, 6, 1491.
- Mills, P. J., et al. (2015). The role of gratitude in spiritual well-being in asymptomatic heart failure patients. Spirituality in Clinical Practice, 2(1), 5–17.
- Wood, A. M., et al. (2010). Gratitude and well-being: A review and theoretical integration. Clinical Psychology Review, 30(7), 890–905.

Chapter 26—Forgiveness: Healing and Releasing the Past

The Story: The Prisoner Who Freed Himself

When James left prison, he carried anger toward those who betrayed him. For years, the bitterness consumed him, until one day, a mentor said: *'You are still imprisoned, not by walls, but by hate.'*

James since began the work of forgiveness. Slowly, the weight lifted, and he became free long before society called him so.

Forgiveness doesn't excuse the wrong; rather, it releases the hold of the past.

Conversation: Mardoche and Karen

Karen: Forgiveness is often misunderstood for it's not forgetting or excusing.

Mardoche: Right. It's freeing yourself from being chained to the hurt.

Karen: At the conscious layer, forgiveness begins with choosing to let go of resentment. At the preconscious layer, it means challenging schemas like 'holding on keeps me safe.' At the unconscious layer, forgiveness requires working through repressed anger and grief. At the existential layer, forgiveness is embracing compassion as a way of being.

Mardoche: Which is why the very best are not those who never get hurt; but those who turn pain into peace.

Science of Forgiveness

1. Health Benefits – Forgiveness reduces stress, lowers blood pressure, and improves immune function (Lawler et al., 2005).

2. Psychological Wellbeing – Forgiveness interventions decrease depression and anxiety (Wade et al., 2014).
3. Neuroscience – Forgiveness activates empathy-related brain circuits (Ricciardi et al., 2013).
4. Relationships – Forgiveness predicts stronger, more lasting bonds (Fincham et al., 2006).
5. Spiritual Growth – Forgiveness is central to most spiritual traditions as a path to freedom.

Case Studies

- Desmond Tutu: Advocated forgiveness through South Africa's Truth and Reconciliation Commission.
- Eva Kor: Holocaust survivor who forgave her tormentors, reclaiming her power.
- Everyday Forgiveness: Friends, families, and partners rebuilding trust.

Toolbox: Practicing Forgiveness

1. Reflection Prompt: What wound am I still carrying that I need to release?
2. Inquiry Exercise: What do I fear will happen if I forgive?
3. Commitment Practice: Write a forgiveness letter (whether or not you send it).

Integration with the 4 Layers of Transformation

- Conscious Layer: Decide to release resentment.
- Preconscious Layer: Challenge schemas of protection through anger.
- Unconscious Layer: Work through repressed pain and grief.
- Existential Layer: Live with compassion as a core stance.

Together: Forgiveness heals the past and unlocks the future.

FORGIVENESS BRIDGE

Closing Narrative

James left prison twice, once through the gates, and once through forgiveness.

The very best are free, not because life spared them hurt, but because they chose to forgive.

References

- Fincham, F. D., et al. (2006). Forgiveness in marriage: Current status and future directions. Family Relations, 55(4), 415–427.
- Lawler, K. A., et al. (2005). A change of heart: Cardiovascular correlates of forgiveness. Journal of Behavioral Medicine, 28(1), 1–11.
- Ricciardi, E., et al. (2013). Neural correlates of forgiveness. Frontiers in Human Neuroscience, 7, 839.
- Wade, N. G., et al. (2014). Effectiveness of forgiveness interventions. Journal of Consulting and Clinical Psychology, 82(1), 154–170.

Chapter 27—Hope: Fuel for the Future

The Story: The Patient Who Believed

Doctors told Anna she had a 10% chance of recovery. She chose to believe she would be among the 10%. Against all odds, she not only survived, but she thrived.

Hope gave her strength science alone could not.

Conversation: Mardoche and Karen

Karen: Hope is not naïve; rather, it's a strategy for survival.

Mardoche: Yes. It's the light that makes people move forward even in the darkest tunnels.

Karen: At the conscious layer, hope looks like goal-setting and planning. At the preconscious layer, it means challenging schemas like 'the future is doomed.' At the unconscious layer, hope softens despair and trauma. At the existential layer, hope is trust in meaning itself, and that life is worth living.

Mardoche: Which is why the very best hold hope not only for themselves, but also for others.

Science of Hope

1. Hope Theory – Snyder (1994) defined hope as agency (willpower) + pathways (plans).
2. Health Outcomes – Hope predicts better recovery from illness (Herth, 2000).
3. Psychological Wellbeing – Hope is linked to resilience, optimism, and lower depression (Gallagher & Lopez, 2009).
4. Education and Performance – Hopeful students achieve more academically (Snyder et al., 2002).

5. Community Hope – Shared hope fosters resilience in groups facing adversity.

Case Studies
- Viktor Frankl: In concentration camps, hope in meaning sustained life.
- Nelson Mandela: Held hope for freedom during 27 years in prison.
- Everyday Hope: Patients, families, and leaders who envision better tomorrows.

Toolbox: Practicing Hope
1. Reflection Prompt: What future possibility keeps me moving forward?
2. Inquiry Exercise: Where do I tell myself 'there's no way'? Can I find at least one pathway?
3. Commitment Practice: Set one meaningful, hopeful goal this month and plan concrete steps.

Integration with the 4 Layers of Transformation
- Conscious Layer: Set goals and create pathways.
- Preconscious Layer: Challenge despair-based schemas.
- Unconscious Layer: Heal despair and trauma through trust.
- Existential Layer: Choose hope as a stance toward life itself.

Together: Hope fuels action, healing, and meaning.

Closing Narrative
Anna survived because she hoped.

The very best don't just predict the future; rather, they also help create it through hope.

References

- Gallagher, M. W., & Lopez, S. J. (2009). Positive expectancies and mental health. Cognitive Therapy and Research, 33(6), 807–816.
- Herth, K. (2000). Enhancing hope in people with a first recurrence of cancer. Journal of Advanced Nursing, 32(6), 1431–1441.
- Snyder, C. R. (1994). The Psychology of Hope. Free Press.
- Snyder, C. R., et al. (2002). Hope theory, academic performance, and well-being. Journal of Educational Psychology, 94(4), 820–826.

Chapter 28—Compassion: The Heart of Greatness

The Story: The Nurse in the Storm

During a hurricane, hospitals overflowed. Amid chaos, a nurse carried food, blankets, and comfort from room to room.

When asked later how she managed, she said: 'I couldn't stop the storm, but I could ease the suffering.'

That's compassion: easing suffering when you cannot erase it.

Conversation: Mardoche and Karen

Karen: Compassion is more than empathy; rather, it's empathy plus action.

Mardoche: Exactly. It's the bridge between feeling another's pain and responding to it.

Karen: At the conscious layer, compassion is daily acts of care. At the preconscious layer, it challenges schemas like 'weakness must be hidden.' At the unconscious layer, compassion helps heal defenses that block connection. At the existential layer, compassion becomes a way of life: honoring the shared humanity in all.

Mardoche: Which is why the very best are not only strong, but kind.

Science of Compassion

1. Health and Stress Reduction – Compassion practices lower stress and increase wellbeing (Pace et al., 2009).
2. Neuroscience – Compassion meditation activates brain regions for empathy and caregiving (Lutz et al., 2008).
3. Relationships – Compassion strengthens trust and intimacy (Crocker & Canevello, 2008).
4. Resilience – Self-compassion fosters recovery from failure (Neff, 2003).
5. Leadership – Compassionate leadership improves morale and performance (Boyatzis et al., 2012).

Case Studies

- Mother Teresa: Embodied compassion through service to the poorest.
- Dalai Lama: Advocates compassion as the foundation of peace.
- Everyday Compassion: Neighbors helping, strangers comforting, families forgiving.

Toolbox: Practicing Compassion

1. Reflection Prompt: Where in my life can I ease someone's suffering today?

2. Inquiry Exercise: What defenses keep me from showing compassion?
3. Commitment Practice: Practice one intentional act of compassion daily.

Integration with the 4 Layers of Transformation
- Conscious Layer: Acts of kindness and care.
- Preconscious Layer: Challenge schemas against vulnerability.
- Unconscious Layer: Heal defenses that block connection.
- Existential Layer: Live as compassion itself.

Together: Compassion transforms suffering into shared humanity.

Closing Narrative

The storm didn't end because of the nurse; but the suffering did.

The very best are remembered not only for their strength, but also for their compassion.

References
- Boyatzis, R. E., et al. (2012). Inspiring sustained commitment to learning. Academy of Management Learning & Education, 11(2), 193–210.
- Crocker, J., & Canevello, A. (2008). Creating and undermining social support in communal relationships. Journal of Personality and Social Psychology, 95(3), 555–575.
- Lutz, A., et al. (2008). Regulation of the neural circuitry of emotion by compassion meditation. PLoS ONE, 3(3), e1897.
- Neff, K. D. (2003). Self-compassion: An alternative conceptualization of a healthy attitude toward oneself. Self and Identity, 2(2), 85–101.
- Pace, T. W., et al. (2009). Effect of compassion meditation on neuroendocrine, innate immune and behavioral responses. Psychoneuroendocrinology, 34(1), 87–98.

Chapter 29—Courageous Conversations: Speaking Truth with Love

The Story: The CEO and the Difficult Talk

When a company crisis hit, the CEO had to face her team. Instead of hiding, she gathered everyone and said: *'Here's the truth: It's tough; but together, we can rebuild.'*

Her honesty didn't weaken trust; rather, it strengthened it.

Courageous conversations are where truth and compassion meet.

Conversation: Mardoche and Karen

Karen: Many people avoid hard conversations out of fear.

Mardoche: Yes. But the best step into them with courage because silence costs more than discomfort.

Karen: At the conscious layer, courageous conversations involve communication skills. At the preconscious layer, they challenge schemas like 'conflict destroys relationships.' At the unconscious layer, they surface repressed fears of rejection. At the existential layer, they become commitments to truth and love as guiding principles.

Mardoche: Which is why the very best are remembered for the hard truths they dared to speak—with kindness.

Science of Courageous Conversations

1. Psychological Safety – Teams that encourage open dialogue perform better (Edmondson, 1999).
2. Health Outcomes – Suppressing emotions and avoiding hard talks increases stress (Gross & Levenson, 1997).
3. Conflict Resolution – Constructive dialogue strengthens relationships (Gottman & Silver, 1999).
4. Leadership – Leaders who engage in difficult conversations build stronger trust (Goleman et al., 2013).
5. Wellbeing – Honest communication fosters authenticity and reduces anxiety.

Case Studies

- Abraham Lincoln: Known for honest yet compassionate speech.
- Brené Brown: Popularized vulnerability as courage in conversations.
- Everyday Courage: Parents addressing conflict, friends telling the truth, leaders facing crises.

Toolbox: Practicing Courageous Conversations
1. Reflection Prompt: What truth am I avoiding sharing right now?
2. Inquiry Exercise: What belief about conflict keeps me silent?
3. Commitment Practice: This week, have one honest conversation you've been postponing.

Integration with the 4 Layers of Transformation
- Conscious Layer: Learn communication and dialogue skills.
- Preconscious Layer: Challenge schemas that avoid conflict.
- Unconscious Layer: Work through fears of rejection and abandonment.
- Existential Layer: Commit to truth and love as life principles.

Together: Courageous conversations transform relationships and cultures.

Closing Narrative
The CEO didn't avoid the storm; rather, she named it.

The very best don't speak to please. They speak to heal, to lead, and to love.

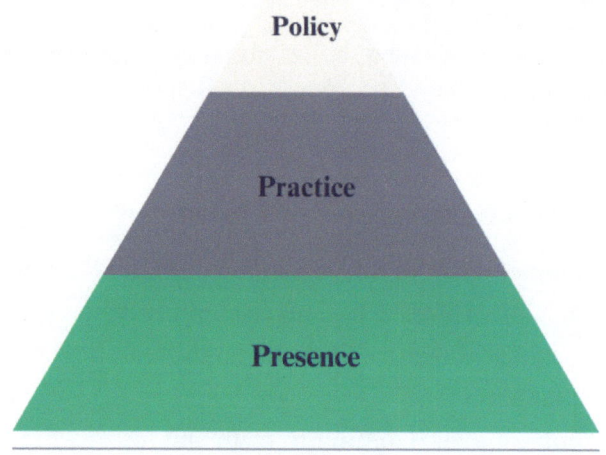

CULTURE SHIFT PYRAMID

References

- Edmondson, A. (1999). Psychological safety and learning behavior in work teams. Administrative Science Quarterly, 44(2), 350–383.
- Goleman, D., Boyatzis, R., & McKee, A. (2013). Primal Leadership. Harvard Business Press.
- Gottman, J., & Silver, N. (1999). The Seven Principles for Making Marriage Work. Crown.
- Gross, J. J., & Levenson, R. W. (1997). Hiding feelings: The acute effects of inhibiting emotion. Journal of Abnormal Psychology, 106(1), 95–103.

Chapter 30—Creativity: Unlocking Human Potential

The Story: The Artist Who Solved Problems

When a village faced water shortages, an artist sketched a design for a rainwater collection system. What began as a drawing became a real solution that transformed lives.

Creativity is not just art; rather, it's the power to imagine and build new possibilities.

Conversation: Mardoche and Karen

Karen: People often think creativity is only for artists.

Mardoche: Yes, but creativity is problem-solving in every field, be it medicine, science, or relationships.

Karen: At the conscious layer, creativity is brainstorming and experimentation. At the preconscious layer, it challenges schemas like 'I'm not creative.' At the unconscious layer, it draws from dreams, free association, and intuition. At the existential layer, creativity is the joy of shaping meaning in the world.

Mardoche: Which is why the very best don't just adapt to reality; rather, they create it.

Science of Creativity

1. Divergent Thinking – Creativity involves generating multiple solutions (Guilford, 1967).
2. Neuroscience – Creative insight activates both hemispheres and the default mode network (Beaty et al., 2016).
3. Resilience – Creative expression helps people cope with trauma (Runco, 2004).

4. Education – Creative problem-solving improves learning outcomes (Robinson, 2011).
5. Wellbeing – Creative activities reduce stress and enhance happiness (Forgeard & Elstein, 2014).

Case Studies
- Steve Jobs: Merged technology with design to revolutionize industries.
- Maya Angelou: Used creativity to heal and inspire through words.
- Everyday Creativity: Parents inventing games, workers innovating solutions, communities reimagining futures.

Toolbox: Practicing Creativity
1. Reflection Prompt: Where in my life do I need a fresh approach?
2. Inquiry Exercise: What assumptions are limiting my imagination?
3. Commitment Practice: Try one creative act daily—writing, doodling, problem-solving, or brainstorming.

Integration with the 4 Layers of Transformation
- Conscious Layer: Experiment and brainstorm solutions.
- Preconscious Layer: Challenge limiting beliefs about creativity.
- Unconscious Layer: Tap into dreams and intuition.
- Existential Layer: Create meaning through acts of imagination.

Together: Creativity is the unlocking of human potential.

Closing Narrative
The artist's sketch brought water to a thirsty village.

The very best don't wait for the future; rather, hey create it.

References

- Beaty, R. E., et al. (2016). Creativity and the default mode network. NeuroImage, 125, 189–206.
- Forgeard, M. J., & Elstein, J. G. (2014). Creativity as a resilience factor. Creativity Research Journal, 26(1), 1–9.
- Guilford, J. P. (1967). The Nature of Human Intelligence. McGraw-Hill.
- Robinson, K. (2011). Out of Our Minds: Learning to be Creative. Capstone.
- Runco, M. A. (2004). Creativity. Annual Review of Psychology, 55, 657–687.

Chapter 31—Presence: The Power of Now

The Story: The Teacher and the Student

A student asked his teacher how to master life. The teacher smiled and said: *'Be here.'*

When the student asked again, the teacher only repeated: *'Be here.'*

Presence is the beginning and the end of mastery.

Conversation: Mardoche and Karen

Karen: Presence is often overlooked because it feels so simple.

Mardoche: Yet it's the hardest practice—to be fully here, without past regrets or future anxieties.

Karen: At the conscious layer, presence comes through mindfulness and grounding practices. At the preconscious layer, it means challenging schemas like 'I'm only valuable when I'm productive.' At the unconscious layer, presence invites repressed emotions to surface in awareness. At the existential layer, presence becomes being itself.

Mardoche: Which is why the very best radiate presence; and you feel it when they walk into the room.

Science of Presence

1. Mindfulness Research – Presence reduces stress, anxiety, and depression (Kabat-Zinn, 2003).
2. Neurobiology – Mindfulness meditation alters brain structure, strengthening attention and emotion regulation (Holzel et al., 2011).
3. Performance – Athletes, performers, and leaders excel when fully present (Csikszentmihalyi, 1990).
4. Relationships – Presence deepens connection, empathy, and intimacy (Carson et al., 2004).

5. Wellbeing – Presence increases joy and meaning by anchoring life in the moment (Brown & Ryan, 2003).

Case Studies

- Eckhart Tolle: Popularized presence as awakening in The Power of Now.
- Jon Kabat-Zinn: Developed MBSR, transforming healthcare with presence practices.
- Everyday Presence: Parents fully listening, friends truly engaging, workers immersed in flow.

Toolbox: Practicing Presence

1. Reflection Prompt: What moments today did I miss because my mind was elsewhere?
2. Inquiry Exercise: What unconscious habit keeps me from being here?
3. Commitment Practice: Set aside 10 minutes daily for presence practice—breathing, noticing, simply being.

Integration with the 4 Layers of Transformation

- Conscious Layer: Practice mindfulness and grounding.
- Preconscious Layer: Challenge productivity-driven schemas.
- Unconscious Layer: Allow hidden emotions to surface.
- Existential Layer: Live as presence itself.

Together: Presence is the essence of transformation.

Closing Narrative

The teacher was right: life is not tomorrow.

The very best live now; and that's why their presence changes everything.

References

- Brown, K. W., & Ryan, R. M. (2003). The benefits of being present. Journal of Personality and Social Psychology, 84(4), 822–848.
- Carson, J. W., et al. (2004). Mindfulness and couples therapy. Journal of Marital and Family Therapy, 30(4), 463–476.
- Csikszentmihalyi, M. (1990). Flow: The Psychology of Optimal Experience. Harper & Row.
- Holzel, B. K., et al. (2011). Mindfulness practice leads to increases in regional brain gray matter density. Psychiatry Research: Neuroimaging, 191(1), 36–43.
- Kabat-Zinn, J. (2003). Mindfulness-based interventions in context. Clinical Psychology: Science and Practice, 10(2), 144–156.

Chapter 32—Resilience: Bounding Forward, Not Just Back

The Story: The Community After the Storm

When a hurricane destroyed homes, the people didn't just rebuild what was lost. They redesigned stronger houses, built community shelters, and created better warning systems.

They didn't just bounce back; rather, they bounced forward.

That is resilience.

Conversation: Mardoche and Karen

Karen: We often think resilience means returning to 'normal.'

Mardoche: But true resilience means transformation; and it's not going back, it's going forward.

Karen: At the conscious layer, resilience looks like healthy coping and habits. At the preconscious layer, it challenges schemas like 'I can't handle setbacks.' At the unconscious layer, it helps heal traumas that weaken adaptation. At the existential layer, resilience is choosing meaning through adversity.

Mardoche: Which is why the very best don't just survive challenges; rather, they grow through them.

Science of Resilience

1. Protective Factors – Social support, optimism, and coping skills predict resilience (Masten, 2001).
2. Neurobiology – Stress inoculation and adaptive plasticity enhance resilience (Southwick & Charney, 2012).
3. Psychology – Resilience predicts lower depression and greater life satisfaction (Bonanno, 2004).

4. Post-Traumatic Growth – Adversity can lead to deeper meaning, stronger relationships, and renewed purpose (Tedeschi & Calhoun, 1996).
5. Community Resilience – Collective resilience fosters recovery after disasters (Norris et al., 2008).

Case Studies
- Holocaust Survivors: Many found resilience in meaning and connection.
- Japanese Communities Post-Tsunami: Demonstrated collective resilience in rebuilding.
- Everyday Resilience: Families facing illness, workers adapting to change, children learning from failure.

Toolbox: Practicing Resilience
1. Reflection Prompt: What past challenge helped me grow stronger?
2. Inquiry Exercise: What limiting belief makes me fear setbacks?
3. Commitment Practice: Build one daily resilience habit (journaling, exercise, gratitude, or reaching out for support).

Integration with the 4 Layers of Transformation
- Conscious Layer: Strengthen coping and habits.
- Preconscious Layer: Challenge helplessness schemas.
- Unconscious Layer: Heal traumas that weaken adaptation.
- Existential Layer: Choose meaning through adversity.

Together: Resilience is transformation through struggle.

Closing Narrative
The storm destroyed homes; but resilience built stronger ones.

The very best don't just endure; rather, they emerge transformed.

References

- Bonanno, G. A. (2004). Loss, trauma, and human resilience. American Psychologist, 59(1), 20–28.
- Masten, A. S. (2001). Ordinary magic: Resilience processes in development. American Psychologist, 56(3), 227–238.
- Norris, F. H., et al. (2008). Community resilience as a metaphor, theory, and set of capacities. American Journal of Community Psychology, 41(1–2), 127–150.
- Southwick, S. M., & Charney, D. S. (2012). The science of resilience: Implications for the prevention and treatment of depression. Science, 338(6103), 79–82.
- Tedeschi, R. G., & Calhoun, L. G. (1996). The Posttraumatic Growth Inventory. Journal of Traumatic Stress, 9(3), 455–471.

Chapter 33—Humility: The Strength of Being Grounded

The Story: The Scientist Who Shared Credit

That brilliant scientist who made that breakthrough discovery. When awarded a prestigious prize, she said: *'This was not my work alone. It was the work of many hands, many minds.'*

Her humility didn't diminish her greatness; rather, it amplified it.

Conversation: Mardoche and Karen

Karen: Humility isn't weakness; rather, it's strength grounded in truth.

Mardoche: Exactly. The best don't need to boast, because their actions speak.

Karen: At the conscious layer, humility means acknowledging limits. At the preconscious layer, it challenges schemas like 'I must always be the best to have value.' At the unconscious layer, humility works through defenses of superiority or inferiority. At the existential layer, humility is choosing interconnectedness over ego.

Mardoche: Which is why the very best inspire not through pride, but through humility.

Science of Humility

1. Psychological Health – Humility predicts greater wellbeing and lower anxiety (Kesebir, 2014).
2. Leadership – Humble leaders foster trust and collaboration (Owens & Hekman, 2012).
3. Relationships – Humility strengthens empathy and forgiveness (Exline & Hill, 2012).
4. Learning – Humility keeps minds open to growth (Tangney, 2000).

5. Spirituality – Humility is central to many wisdom traditions as a pathway to wisdom.

Case Studies
- Nelson Mandela: Led with humility, lifting others' voices.
- Mother Teresa: Chose service over recognition.
- Everyday Humility: Parents apologizing to children, leaders sharing credit, friends admitting mistakes.

Toolbox: Practicing Humility
1. Reflection Prompt: Where have I mistaken pride for strength?
2. Inquiry Exercise: What belief keeps me from admitting I don't know?
3. Commitment Practice: Share credit today with someone who helped you succeed.

Integration with the 4 Layers of Transformation
- Conscious Layer: Practice acknowledgment of limits.
- Preconscious Layer: Challenge schemas that tie value to superiority.
- Unconscious Layer: Work through defenses of arrogance or shame.
- Existential Layer: Choose connection and wisdom over ego.

Together: Humility is the ground where true greatness grows.

Closing Narrative

The scientist's humility didn't hide her brilliance; rather, it revealed her character.

The very best are not the loudest; rather, they are the humblest.

References

- Exline, J. J., & Hill, P. C. (2012). Humility: A consistent and robust predictor of generosity. The Journal of Positive Psychology, 7(3), 208–218.
- Kesebir, P. (2014). A quiet ego: Psychological wellbeing and humility. Journal of Positive Psychology, 9(5), 360–371.
- Owens, B. P., & Hekman, D. R. (2012). Modeling how to grow: An inductive examination of humble leader behaviors. Academy of Management Journal, 55(4), 787–818.
- Tangney, J. P. (2000). Humility: Theoretical perspectives, empirical findings, and directions for future research. Journal of Social and Clinical Psychology, 19(1), 70–82.

Chapter 34—Vision: Seeing Beyond the Present

The Story: The Farmer Who Planted Trees

A farmer planted hundreds of trees, knowing they would not bear fruit for decades. When asked why, he said: *'I plant not for myself, but for my grandchildren.'*

Vision is the ability to see what is not yet here, and to act as if it already exists.

Conversation: Mardoche and Karen

Karen: Visionaries are sometimes misunderstood for they see what others cannot yet see.

Mardoche: Exactly. The best leaders, teachers, and healers act from vision, not just from the present.

Karen: At the conscious layer, vision is setting goals. At the preconscious layer, it means challenging schemas like 'the future will only repeat the past.' At the unconscious layer, vision draws from imagination, dreams, and archetypes. At the existential layer, vision is choosing to live toward one's ultimate purpose.

Mardoche: Which is why the very best create the future before others even glimpse it.

Science of Vision

1. Leadership Studies – Visionary leadership predicts higher engagement and performance (Kirkpatrick & Locke, 1996).
2. Neuroscience of Imagination – Future thinking activates the same brain networks as memory (Schacter et al., 2012).
3. Psychology of Hope – Vision enhances motivation and persistence (Snyder, 2002).

4. Education & Organizations – Shared vision improves teamwork and outcomes (Boyatzis & Akrivou, 2006).
5. Resilience – A clear vision fosters perseverance through adversity.

Case Studies
- Martin Luther King Jr.: His vision of equality transformed nations.
- Elon Musk: Pursued visions of space travel and renewable energy against skepticism.
- Everyday Visionaries: Parents dreaming for their children, communities planning for generations.

Toolbox: Practicing Vision
1. Reflection Prompt: What future possibility calls to me most deeply?
2. Inquiry Exercise: What limiting belief keeps me from imagining boldly?
3. Commitment Practice: Write one vision statement for your life and identify one step you can take today toward it.

Integration with the 4 Layers of Transformation
- Conscious Layer: Goal-setting and planning.
- Preconscious Layer: Challenge schemas that limit imagination.
- Unconscious Layer: Draw on archetypes, dreams, and symbols.
- Existential Layer: Live toward ultimate purpose.

Together: Vision expands reality into possibility.

Closing Narrative
The farmer's trees will bear fruit for grandchildren he will never meet.

The very best live for visions larger than themselves.

References

- Boyatzis, R. E., & Akrivou, K. (2006). The ideal self as the driver of intentional change. Journal of Management Development, 25(7), 624–642.
- Kirkpatrick, S. A., & Locke, E. A. (1996). Direct and indirect effects of three core charismatic leadership components. Leadership Quarterly, 7(1), 1–33.
- Schacter, D. L., et al. (2012). The future of memory: Remembering, imagining, and the brain. Neuron, 76(4), 677–694.
- Snyder, C. R. (2002). Hope theory: Rainbows in the mind. Psychological Inquiry, 13(4), 249–275.

Chapter 35 Unity Beyond the Self

The Story: The Broken Sticks

A teacher gave each student a single stick and asked them to break it. All snapped easily. Then he gave them a bundle of sticks tied together, and no one could break it.

"Alone, we are fragile," he said. "Together, unbreakable."

Unity is strength beyond the individual.

Conversation: Mardoche and Karen

Karen: Unity isn't sameness; rather, it's harmony among differences.

Mardoche: Exactly. The very best don't erase individuality; rather, they weave it into wholeness.

Karen: At the conscious layer, unity is teamwork and collaboration. At the preconscious layer, it challenges schemas like 'I must do it alone.' At the unconscious layer, unity heals fears of rejection and isolation. At the existential layer, unity is recognizing that we are one human family.

Mardoche: Which is why the very best are bridge-builders, not dividers.

Science of Unity

1. Social Psychology – Belonging is a fundamental human need (Baumeister & Leary, 1995).
2. Neuroscience – Social connection activates reward circuits and reduces pain perception (Eisenberger, 2013).
3. Health – Unity and belonging protect against depression and increase longevity (Holt-Lunstad et al., 2015).
4. Leadership – Unified teams are more resilient, creative, and effective.

5. Global Perspective – Unity across nations and groups is essential for peace and progress.

Case Studies

- The U.S. Civil Rights Movement: Unity across races strengthened progress.
- South Africa's Truth and Reconciliation Commission: Unity made healing possible.
- Everyday Unity: Families, workplaces, communities choosing to come together.

Toolbox: Practicing Unity

1. Reflection Prompt: Where am I dividing instead of uniting?
2. Inquiry Exercise: What belief keeps me from asking for or offering support?
3. Commitment Practice: Take one step to build unity today—repair a conflict, strengthen a team, or collaborate.

Integration with the 4 Layers of Transformation
- Conscious Layer: Practice teamwork and collaboration.
- Preconscious Layer: Challenge schemas of isolation.
- Unconscious Layer: Heal rejection and loneliness wounds.
- Existential Layer: Live in awareness of our shared humanity.

Together: Unity makes us unbreakable.

Closing Narrative
The bundle of sticks could not be broken.

The very best know that beyond the self lies strength in unity.

References
- Baumeister, R. F., & Leary, M. R. (1995). The need to belong: Desire for interpersonal attachments as a fundamental human motivation. Psychological Bulletin, 117(3), 497–529.
- Eisenberger, N. I. (2013). Social ties and health: A social neuroscience perspective. Current Directions in Psychological Science, 22(3), 123–129.
- Holt-Lunstad, J., et al. (2015). Loneliness and social isolation as risk factors for mortality: A meta-analytic review. Perspectives on Psychological Science, 10(2), 227–237.

Part VI: The Circle of Transformation

Chapter 36—The Circle of Transformation

The Story: The Four Gates

Amara, a young woman, felt a restless emptiness. One night, she dreamed of a circle of light with four gates, each marked by a symbol. A voice whispered: *'Walk the circle, and you will find your true self.'*

At dawn, she began her journey.

Conversation: Mardoche and Karen

Karen: The Circle of Transformation is the essence of human growth.

Mardoche: Yes. The very best don't simply change habits; rather, they move through all four layers—conscious, preconscious, unconscious, and existential.

Karen: At the conscious level, we begin with structure and practice. At the preconscious, we re-examine schemas and patterns. At the unconscious, we unearth what was buried. And at the existential, we embrace freedom and meaning.

Mardoche: Which is why transformation is not linear; rather, it is a circle; and we return again and again, each time deeper.

Circle of Transformation

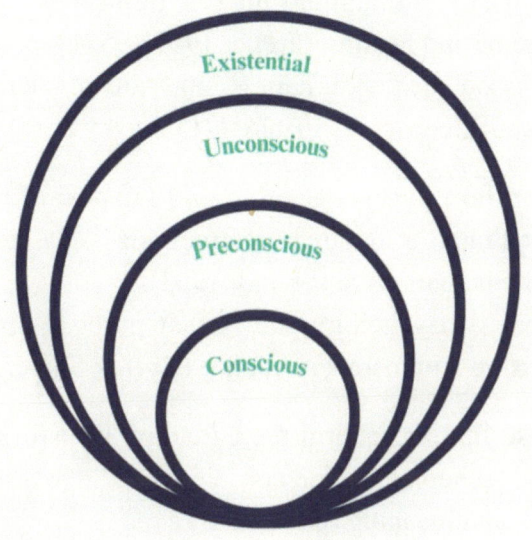

Science of Transformation

Research confirms that growth unfolds across layers of mind and being:

1. **Conscious Layer – Habits and Behavior**
   - Behavior change requires consistency, accountability, and environmental support (Lally et al., 2010).
   - Mindfulness and breathing practices regulate stress and improve executive function (Tang et al., 2015).

2. **Preconscious Layer – Schemas and Beliefs**
   - Core beliefs and schemas guide perception and behavior; schema therapy shows restructuring them improves outcomes for chronic conditions (Young et al., 2003).
   - Attachment theory demonstrates how early patterns shape relational schemas that can be reworked (Mikulincer & Shaver, 2016).

3. **Unconscious Layer – Repressed Material**
   - Psychoanalysis highlights the role of unconscious conflicts in symptoms and healing (Freud, 1915/1957).
   - Free association, journaling, and dream analysis increase access to unconscious material (Luborsky & Barrett, 2007).

4. **Existential Layer – Meaning and Purpose**
   - Viktor Frankl's logotherapy emphasizes that meaning is the ultimate human drive (Frankl, 1963).
   - Existential psychology shows that purpose protects against depression and fosters resilience (Ryff & Singer, 1998).

Together, these findings affirm the Circle of Transformation: habits (conscious), schemas (preconscious), repressed content (unconscious), and meaning (existential).

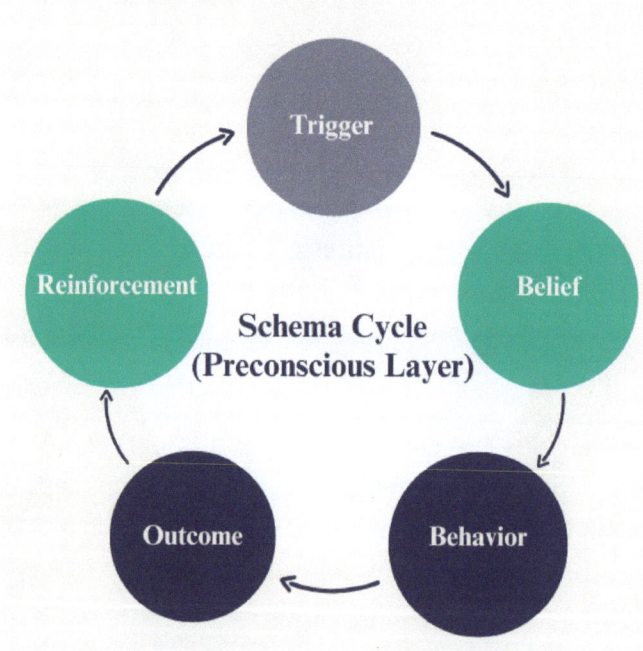

Case Studies
- Nelson Mandela – Cultivated discipline (conscious), re-examined beliefs (preconscious), confronted trauma of imprisonment (unconscious), and emerged with a vision of reconciliation (existential).
- A patient in schema therapy – Began with daily mindfulness practice (conscious), uncovered a schema of 'I am unlovable' (preconscious), processed childhood neglect (unconscious), and created a purposeful life in service to others (existential).
- Everyday Life – A parent develops healthier routines (conscious), challenges beliefs of inadequacy (preconscious), processes grief (unconscious), and embraces parenting as a sacred calling (existential).

Toolbox: Practicing the Circle of Transformation
1. Reflection Prompt: Which gate of the circle am I standing at today?
2. Inquiry Exercise: What pattern, belief, or shadow am I being asked to face?
3. Commitment Practice: Take one action in each layer this week:
    - Conscious: Build one new habit.
    - Preconscious: Challenge one unhelpful schema.
    - Unconscious: Journal or reflect on a dream.
    - Existential: Clarify one value or purpose.

Integration with the Four Layers of Transformation
- Conscious Layer: Habits and behavior—discipline, mindfulness, self-care.
- Preconscious Layer: Schemas and beliefs—reshaping narratives and attachments.
- Unconscious Layer: Repressed material—uncovering and integrating hidden wounds.

- Existential Layer: Meaning and purpose—choosing freedom, responsibility, and love.

Together, they form the Circle of Transformation—a lifelong return to deeper wholeness.

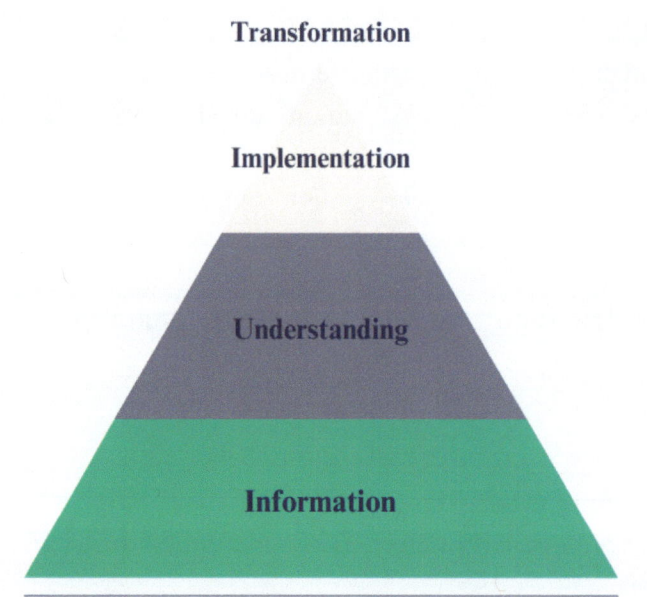

FROM INFORMATION TO TRANSFORMATION

Closing Narrative

Amara returned to her village, carrying no treasure but walking with presence. She smiled as others asked what had changed.

'I walked the Circle of Transformation,' she said.

Her life itself was the answer.

References

- Frankl, V. E. (1963). Man's Search for Meaning. Beacon Press.
- Freud, S. (1957). The Unconscious. In J. Strachey (Ed.), The Standard Edition of the Complete Psychological Works of Sigmund Freud (Vol. 14, pp. 159–215). (Original work published 1915).
- Lally, P., van Jaarsveld, C. H. M., Potts, H. W. W., & Wardle, J. (2010). How are habits formed: Modelling habit formation in the real world. European Journal of Social Psychology, 40(6), 998–1009.
- Luborsky, L., & Barrett, M. S. (2007). The history and empirical status of key psychoanalytic concepts. Annual Review of Clinical Psychology, 3, 1–21.
- Mikulincer, M., & Shaver, P. R. (2016). Attachment in Adulthood: Structure, Dynamics, and Change (2nd ed.). Guilford Press.
- Ryff, C. D., & Singer, B. (1998). The contours of positive human health. Psychological Inquiry, 9(1), 1–28.
- Tang, Y.-Y., Hölzel, B. K., & Posner, M. I. (2015). The neuroscience of mindfulness meditation. Nature Reviews Neuroscience, 16(4), 213–225.
- Young, J. E., Klosko, J. S., & Weishaar, M. E. (2003). Schema Therapy: A Practitioner's Guide. Guilford Press.

Conclusion: Living the Circle

Every page of this book has carried you deeper into the question that began it all: What makes the very best?

The answer is not found in talent, luck, or circumstance. It is found in the willingness to walk the Circle of Transformation, through practice, through belief, through shadow, and into meaning. The very best are not those who avoid struggle, but those who embrace growth. They are not those who never fall, but those who rise with greater wisdom each time. They are not those who live for themselves, but those who live in service to something larger.

The Four Layers of Transformation remind us that greatness is both practical and profound:

- At the conscious layer, it begins with habits, discipline, and daily practices.
- At the preconscious layer, it continues with the courage to examine and rewrite old patterns.
- At the unconscious layer, it deepens with the healing of what has long been hidden.
- At the existential layer, it culminates in freedom, meaning, and purpose.

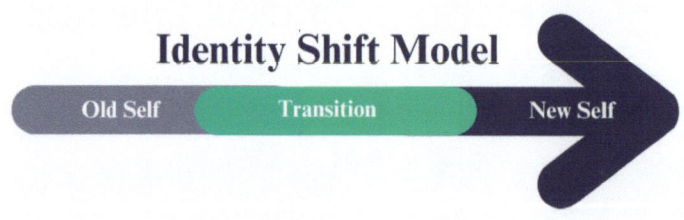

And then the circle returns—because each layer ought to be revisited again and again, at every stage of life.

The chapters on courage, gratitude, compassion, wisdom, resilience, love, and service remind us that greatness is not abstract; rather, it is embodied in virtues lived daily. The very best are not defined by their achievements but by the way they show up, which is with presence, integrity, and heart.

If there is one lesson this book leaves with you, let it be this: the very best is not something out there; rather, it is something already within you, waiting to be practiced, remembered, and lived.

This is not the end of the process; rather, the beginning of a new cycle. As you close these pages, may you open the next chapter of your own life, walking the circle, practicing the virtues, and living as the very best version of yourself.

Epilogue: You Were Always Enough

The circle is complete.

You have walked through discipline and practice, through patterns and beliefs, through shadows and depths, into freedom and meaning. You have explored the virtues of greatness—love, courage, gratitude, resilience, wisdom—and perhaps you have discovered what we discovered: that the very best is not a destination but a way of being.

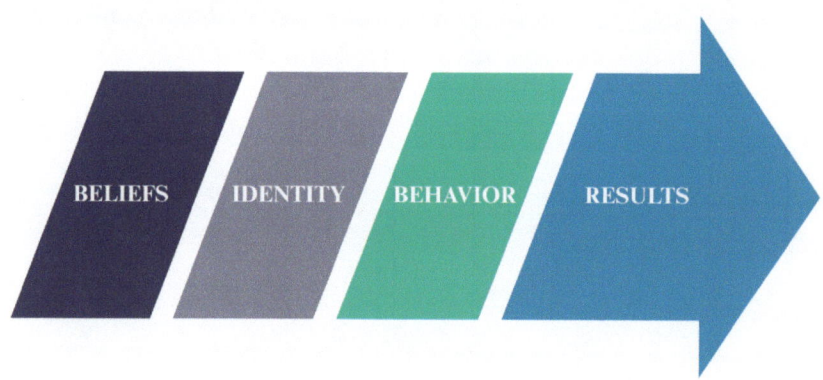

The process does not end here. The Circle of Transformation is not a single path to be walked once; rather, it is a rhythm, a return, and an invitation you will hear again and again. Each time, the circle widens, each time, you discover new depths of who you are and new heights of what you can bring to the world.

If there is one truth we hope you carry from these pages, it is this: you were always enough. Greatness is not something to be earned or achieved; rather, it is something to be remembered, uncovered, and lived. The whisper you heard at the beginning, the call to become the very best, was never about becoming someone else; rather, it was about becoming fully yourself.

So as you close this book, remember: the work is not over, because life is never finished teaching us. Return to the practices, return to the circle, and return to the simple acts of presence, compassion, and courage that make you the very best, and not for applause, not for recognition, but because this is who you are.

The circle is yours now.

Step into it, again and again.

And may you live as the very best version of yourself, because the world needs nothing less.

Invitation to the Reader

You have reached the final page of this book, but the process is not over; rather, it is only beginning. Further, the Circle of Transformation is not meant to sit on paper; rather, it is meant to live in you, to breathe in your choices, and to shine in your presence.

Pause for a moment, and reflect on what stirred you most as you read:

- What insight do you want to carry forward?
- What practice do you want to commit to today?
- What meaning or purpose do you want to claim as your own?

Write it down, share it with someone you trust, and begin living it now.

Greatness is not a solitary path, and transformation deepens when it is shared. So, tell your story, invite others to walk the circle with you. In doing so, you not only grow; rather, you become part of the growth of others.

If this book has touched you, we ask one final thing: share it. Share it with a colleague, a friend, a loved one. If it has made a difference in your life, please take a moment to leave a review. Reviews are more than feedback; rather, they are acts of service, and a way of helping others discover a path that may change their lives too.

The circle is now yours. May you walk it with courage. May you return to it with humility; and may you live it with love.

May you also remember, always that you were meant to be the very best.

Final Acknowledgments

As we close this book, we pause to recognize that no work of this magnitude is ever accomplished alone. The Circle of Transformation we describe here has been lived not just by us, but with us, by the people who stood beside us, challenged us, believed in us, and walked the path together.

We thank our colleagues and collaborators at the SWEET Institute. Your dedication to learning, growing, and practicing transformation has been both the testing ground and the inspiration for this work. You have shown us, again and again, that when a community commits to growth, lives change, and not only for clinicians but for every person they serve.

We thank the clinicians, leaders, and seekers who shared their stories with us. Your courage to be vulnerable, to speak truth, and to pursue wholeness has given this book its heartbeat.

We thank our families, who have carried us with love and patience throughout the writing process. You are our foundation, our reminder of what matters most, and our teachers in the everyday practice of presence, humility, and love.

We thank our mentors and teachers, past and present, who instilled in us the conviction that knowledge without compassion is incomplete, and compassion without action is insufficient. Your wisdom lives in these pages.

And finally, we thank you, the reader. You are the reason this book exists. Your courage to step into the circle, to live more fully, to practice transformation, is what makes these words alive. This book is not complete without your story, your practice, your contribution.

May the acknowledgments here serve as a reminder: greatness is never solitary. It is always shared. In this vein, we close with gratitude—for every hand, every heart, and every life that has joined us in making this work possible.

With love and thanks,

Mardoche Sidor, MD
Karen Dubin, PhD, LCSW

Reader Integration Toolkit: From Message to Implementation

This toolkit is designed to help you take the wisdom from each chapter and put it into daily practice. Transformation happens not in what we read, but in what we live. Use these tools as a bridge from message to implementation, from insight to action, and from theory to transformation.

1. The Circle of Transformation Daily Tracker

Use this to check in with each layer every day.

Conscious Layer: What one action will I commit to today (exercise, nutrition, sleep, breath, structure)?

Did I follow through? ☐ Yes ☐ No

Preconscious Layer: What limiting belief or pattern showed up today?

How did I reframe it?

Unconscious Layer: What emotion, dream, or hidden thought surfaced today?

How did I honor or process it?

Existential Layer: What meaning or purpose guided my choices today?

Did I live aligned with that purpose?

2. Weekly Reflection Prompts

- What was the most important lesson I practiced this week?
- Which chapter's message was hardest to implement? Why?
- Where did I notice growth or resilience?

- Where did I fall short—and how can I return to the circle with compassion?
- What is my intention for the coming week?

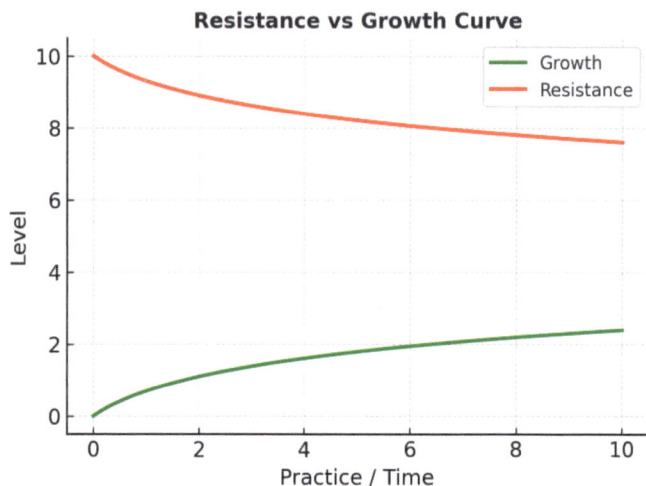

3. Toolbox of Practices by Virtue

Match each chapter to a daily exercise:

- Courage (Ch. 14): Take one small action today that scares you. Write down what happened.
- Gratitude (Ch. 25): List three things you are grateful for and share one with another person.
- Compassion (Ch. 28): Offer yourself one phrase of self-compassion, and one compassionate act to someone else.
- Wisdom (Ch. 20): Ask yourself: What do I need to see differently today?
- Presence (Ch. 18 & 31): Pause for one minute of mindful breathing before beginning a task.

4. Integration Journaling Template

Use this template to connect each chapter's message into your own circle of transformation:

Chapter I Am Working On: _____

Insight I Gained: _____

Tool I Practiced: _____

What Changed (Behavior / Belief / Awareness / Purpose): _____

How I Will Carry This Forward: _____

5. Commitment Contract

I commit to walking the Circle of Transformation—not once, but as a way of life. I will practice daily, question patterns, face what is hidden, and live with meaning. I will return to this circle with courage, humility, and love.

Signature: _____

Date: _____

Appendix: Tools, Exercises, Charts, and Frameworks

This appendix brings together the core practices and frameworks introduced in the book. Use it as a quick reference and as a practical guide to return to daily, weekly, or whenever you need to anchor yourself in the Circle of Transformation.

A. The Four Layers of Transformation Framework

Layer	Focus	Practices & Tools
Conscious	Habits, routines, behavior	Sleep hygiene, exercise, breath awareness, meditation, mindful eating, daily structure
Preconscious	Schemas, beliefs, patterns	Schema journaling, mindfulness of thought patterns, reframing exercises, attachment reflection
Unconscious	Repressed memories, defenses, shadow	Dream analysis, free association journaling, defense identification, transference reflection
Existential	Freedom, meaning, purpose	Values clarification, purpose mapping, Golden Rule compass, meaning-making exercises

B. The Circle of Transformation Chart

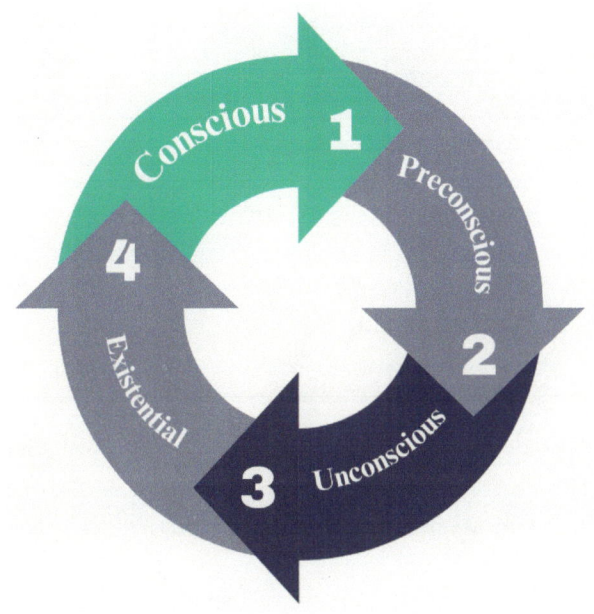

C. Daily and Weekly Practice Tools
Daily Tracker:

- Conscious: My one daily action: _____

- Preconscious: Belief or schema I noticed: _____

- Unconscious: Hidden thought/emotion surfaced: _____

- Existential: Meaning guiding me today: _____

Weekly Reflection:

- Lesson I practiced most: _____

- Challenge I faced: _____

- Growth I noticed: _____

- Intention for next week: _____

Weekly Reflection Table

Day	Lesson	Challenge	Growth	Intention
Mon				
Tue				
Wed				
Thu				
Fri				
Sat				
Sun				

D. Toolbox by Virtue (Chapter Practices)

Courage: Take one small action today that scares you.

Gratitude: Write down 3 things you're grateful for and share one.

Compassion: Offer a phrase of self-compassion and one act of compassion outward.

Resilience: Write down one setback this week and the lesson it carried.

Presence: Pause for 3 conscious breaths before each transition today.

Wisdom: Ask: What is the deeper lesson here?

E. Exercises for Deeper Integration

1. Schema Reframing Worksheet – Identify an old belief, reframe it, write new action aligned with the reframed belief.
2. Unconscious Exploration Exercise – Free write for 10 minutes without editing; circle recurring words; reflect on what is surfacing.
3. Existential Alignment Exercise – Write your top 3 values. For each, list one action you can take this week to live in alignment.

F. Commitment Contract

I commit to walking the Circle of Transformation—not once, but as a way of life. I will practice daily, question patterns, face what is hidden, and live with meaning. I will return to this circle with courage, humility, and love.

Signature: _____

Date: _____

Commitment Contract

I, _____

Commit to _____

Starting on: _____

Signature: _____

Recommended Reading

On Habits, Discipline, and Daily Practice (Conscious Layer)
- James Clear – Atomic Habits
- Charles Duhigg – The Power of Habit
- Jon Kabat-Zinn – Wherever You Go, There You Are
- Andrew Huberman – Protocols for Daily Practice (Huberman Lab resources)

On Patterns, Schemas, and Beliefs (Preconscious Layer)
- Jeffrey Young, Janet Klosko – Reinventing Your Life
- Daniel Kahneman – Thinking, Fast and Slow
- Carol Dweck – Mindset: The New Psychology of Success
- Bessel van der Kolk – The Body Keeps the Score

On the Unconscious and the Hidden Self
- Sigmund Freud – The Interpretation of Dreams
- Carl Jung – Man and His Symbols
- Irvin Yalom – The Gift of Therapy
- Adam Phillips – On Kissing, Tickling, and Being Bored

On Freedom, Meaning, and the Existential Layer
- Viktor Frankl – Man's Search for Meaning
- Rollo May – Love and Will
- Martin Seligman – Flourish
- Parker Palmer – Let Your Life Speak

On Virtues, Values, and Human Flourishing
- Brené Brown – Daring Greatly
- Kristin Neff – Self-Compassion
- Dalai Lama & Desmond Tutu – The Book of Joy
- Stephen Covey – The 7 Habits of Highly Effective People

On Integration and Presence
- Eckhart Tolle – The Power of Now
- Thich Nhat Hanh – The Miracle of Mindfulness
- Michael Singer – The Untethered Soul
- Pema Chödrön – When Things Fall Apart

References

- Brown, B. (2012). Daring greatly: How the courage to be vulnerable transforms the way we live, love, parent, and lead. Gotham Books.
- Chödrön, P. (1997). When things fall apart: Heart advice for difficult times. Shambhala Publications.
- Clear, J. (2018). Atomic habits: An easy & proven way to build good habits & break bad ones. Avery.
- Covey, S. R. (1989). The 7 habits of highly effective people. Free Press.
- Duhigg, C. (2012). The power of habit: Why we do what we do in life and business. Random House.
- Dweck, C. S. (2006). Mindset: The new psychology of success. Random House.
- Frankl, V. E. (2006). *Man's search for meaning*. Beacon Press. (Original work published 1946)
- Freud, S. (2010). *The interpretation of dreams*. Basic Books. (Original work published 1900)
- Jung, C. G. (1964). *Man and his symbols*. Doubleday.
- Kabat-Zinn, J. (1994). Wherever you go, there you are: Mindfulness meditation in everyday life. Hyperion.
- Kahneman, D. (2011). *Thinking, fast and slow*. Farrar, Straus and Giroux.
- May, R. (1969). *Love and will*. W. W. Norton & Company.
- Neff, K. (2011). Self-compassion: The proven power of being kind to yourself. William Morrow.
- Palmer, P. J. (2000). Let your life speak: Listening for the voice of vocation. Jossey-Bass.
- Phillips, A. (1993). On kissing, tickling, and being bored: Psychoanalytic essays on the unexamined life. Harvard University Press.

- Seligman, M. E. P. (2011). Flourish: A visionary new understanding of happiness and well-being. Free Press.
- Singer, M. A. (2007). *The untethered soul: The journey beyond yourself.* New Harbinger Publications.
- Tolle, E. (1999). The power of now: A guide to spiritual enlightenment. New World Library.
- van der Kolk, B. (2014). The body keeps the score: Brain, mind, and body in the healing of trauma. Viking.
- Young, J. E., & Klosko, J. S. (1993). Reinventing your life: The breakthrough program to end negative behavior and feel great again. Plume.
- Yalom, I. D. (2002). The gift of therapy: An open letter to a new generation of therapists and their patients. HarperCollins.

More from SWEET Institute Publishing

At SWEET Institute Publishing, we believe books are more than words on a page. They are tools for transformation; and each book is designed to bridge science and practice, knowledge and integration, and story and action.

We invite you to explore more titles from our growing library:

On Transformation and Healing
- Before Anything Else, Validate
- Breaking the Pattern: Understanding and Healing Repetition Compulsion
- Freeing Fear: A Journey Through the Mind – Conscious, Preconscious, and Unconscious
- The Circle of Transformation

On Clinician Growth and Practice
- The Courage to Care: Stories of Healing, Hope, and the Power of Social Work
- Reflections: The Clinician's Mirror
- The Existential Clinician
- Redefining Psychoanalysis

On Life, Presence, and Power
- How Life Works
- The Kindness Imperative: How Power Becomes Purpose, and Why True Greatness Begins with Grace
- The Simplicity Principle
- The Still Point

On Community and System Change

- The Anchor Blueprint: Redefining Care for the Forgotten, the Misunderstood, and the High Acuity
- Nou Se Peyi A
- Because of Us

To learn more, join our newsletter and explore upcoming titles at:

www.SweetInstitutePublishing.com

Every book is an invitation. Every page is a step on the circle. Together, we are building a transformational world.

About the Authors

Mardoche Sidor, MD

Dr. Mardoche Sidor is a Harvard- and Columbia-trained psychiatrist, quadruple board-certified in General Psychiatry, Child and Adolescent Psychiatry, Forensic Psychiatry, and Addiction Psychiatry. He also completed advanced training in Public and Community Psychiatry and Geriatric Psychiatry.

He is the Founder of the SWEET Institute (Supporting Wellbeing through Empowerment, Education, and Training), a global community dedicated to bridging science, practice, and transformation for clinicians and leaders. Dr. Sidor currently serves as Medical Director at Urban Pathways, one of New York City's leading supportive housing organizations, where he leads innovative models of care for individuals experiencing homelessness, serious mental illness, substance use, trauma, and systemic marginalization. His current academic affiliation is Columbia University Center for Psychoanalytic Study and Research.

Dr. Sidor is a prolific author and visionary educator. Through SWEET Institute Publishing, he is building a transformational library of books that integrate science, story, and practice, making knowledge actionable for clinicians and everyday seekers alike. His mission is simple but profound: to light the path home—one person, one community, one circle of transformation at a time.

Karen Dubin, Ph.D., LCSW

Dr. Karen Dubin is a social worker, educator, and writer whose career has centered on integrating research, practice, and the lived human experience. With a background in both education and social work, she has worked extensively in community mental health, higher education, criminal justice, and organizational leadership.

As Co-Founder of the SWEET Institute, and Director of Publishing and Co-Author at the SWEET Institute Publishing, Dr. Dubin has helped shape an educational model that bridges intellectual understanding with experiential learning and lasting behavioral change. She has co-authored dozens of SWEET Institute publications and is a pioneering voice in advancing narrative, presence-based approaches to clinical care.

Karen's writing weaves together science, story, and reflection, inviting readers and clinicians alike to step beyond knowledge into wisdom. Her commitment is to help individuals and organizations live into their values, deepen their practice, and embody transformation.

Together

Mardoche and Karen co-create at the intersection of science, story, and soul. Their shared vision is to move the mental health and social service fields, and the world at large, from information to transformation, and from surviving to fully living.

www.ingramcontent.com/pod-product-compliance
Lightning Source LLC
Chambersburg PA
CBHW041611220426
43669CB00001B/1